GARY SPEED

REMEMBERED

First published in 2012 by
André Deutsch
an imprint of the
Carlton Publishing Group
20 Mortimer Street
London W1T 3JW

Text copyright © Paul Abbandonato 2012
Design copyright © Carlton Books Limited 2012

The publishers would like to thank the following sources for their kind permission to reproduce the pictures in this book.

Plate Section
Page 1: (both) collects supplied by Mirrorpix. Page 2: (both) Bob Thomas/Getty Images. Page 3: (top) Clive Brunskill/Getty Images; (bottom) Getty Images. Page 4: (top) Stu Forster/ Getty Images; (bottom) Steve Parkin/AFP/Getty Images. Page 5: Michael Steele/Getty Images. Page 6: (top) Matthew Lewis/Getty Images; (bottom) Jamie McDonald/Getty Images. Page 7: (both) Michael Regan/Getty Images. Page 8: (top) Gareth Copley/Getty Images; (centre) Julian Finney/Getty Images; (bottom) Clive Mason/Getty Images.

Every effort has been made to acknowledge correctly and contact the source and/or copyright holder of each picture and Carlton Books Limited apologizes for any unintentional errors or omissions which will be corrected in future editions of this book.

Designer: Harj Ghundale
Copyeditor: Jane Donovan
Proofreader: Lesley Levene
Indexer: Colin Hynson
Project Editor: Matthew Lowing

Can't Take My Eyes Off You by Bob Crewe and Bob Gaudio reprinted by permission of EMI Music Publishing

A CIP catalogue for this book is available from the British Library.

ISBN 978 1 233 00365 8

Printed and bound in Great Britain by CPI Group (UK) Ltd, Croydon CR0 4YY

GARY
SPEED
REMEMBERED

Paul Abbandonato

ANDRE
DEUTSCH

Acknowledgements

Those I approached for help in writing this book could not have been more accommodating. My thanks go to, among others, his former managers Howard Wilkinson, Sam Allardyce, Terry Yorath and Bobby Gould, who each spoke so glowingly about Gary. So too his friend and agent Hayden Evans, Wales coach Osian Roberts and Welsh FA chief executive Jonathan Ford, who were left to pick up the professional pieces once some of the shock surrounding his death had begun to subside. Kevin McCabe, the Sheffield United chairman who handed Gary his first management job, gave me a wonderful insight into the qualities he spotted early which made Speedo a top boss in the making.

My thanks also go to Ceri Stennett, Roger Gibbins, Gary Cooper (Leeds supporters group), Mark Jensen (Newcastle supporters group), my employer MediaWales, and in particular my Editor Alan Edmunds for his help over the years. And Carlton, of course, for coming up with the book project in the first place. Matthew Lowing, in particular, has been a great help to me with his advice and guidance.

Last, but by no means least, my thanks also to my lovely wife, Paula, and my three wonderful children, Ben, Sam and Joe, for their time, patience and understanding as I processed these words, making the home computer my sole domain and thus, in doing so, denying them the opportunity to chat to their many friends on Facebook!

That all said, I guess the man we should all really be thanking is Gary Andrew Speed, who enriched the lives of so many who came across him.

Contents

Introduction

It is with something of a heavy heart and a tinge of sadness that I write these words. Gary Andrew Speed was one of life's true gentlemen and the events of November 27, 2011, when the news of his sudden death at just 42 years of age was announced, still leave many of us numb with shock. Football has, without doubt, lost one of its finest role models.

I count myself fortunate to have known Gary, or "Speedo" as he was called by those of us friendly with him, for more than 20 years in my capacity as head of sport and leading football writer on Wales's national newspapers, the *Western Mail* and *Wales on Sunday*. Others may have been closer to him but few would have had as many professional dealings as I did over a two-decade period, which began when he was an unknown teenager from north Wales and starting to make his mark with Leeds United, right through to those final days as manager of Wales. Therefore I can tell you from first-hand experience that his attributes, both as a football player, a manager, and, perhaps more importantly, a human being were perhaps too numerous to mention. To try and sum it up as best I can, he was amiable, courteous, dignified, gracious and approachable. In all the time I knew him, he never once, not once, rejected a request for an interview. His kindness and diplomatic nature made him the perfect ambassador to captain his country with such distinction for seven years and then, almost inevitably, to become manager of Wales, too.

This book is a celebration of Gary Speed's life and incredible career as one of the truly great modern-day British footballers, who went on to become manager of Wales, a job which, as a proud Welshman, he described as "the greatest honour I could have". He performed the role magnificently, too: his young charges, inspired by Gareth Bale, Aaron Ramsey and the one old head Craig Bellamy but strongly moulded together by their much-loved manager, rocketing up the FIFA rankings with a world-record rise in 2011.

Speedo seemed to have so much to look forward to in 2012, when the World Cup qualifying campaign for Brazil 2014 would begin. A Welsh nation, fragmented in football terms for too long, had been reunited by this one man and given fresh hope, vibrancy, buoyancy and optimism. He was the person to end a qualifying jinx dating back to the Dragons Class of 1958, the last Wales team to reach a major finals, we felt. Quite what set of circumstances led to him being found hanged on the steps leading down to the garage of his Cheshire home, shared with wife, Louise, and sons, Edward and Thomas, we may never know but his tragic passing on that dark day caused an outpouring of grief, the scale of which is rarely seen in this country. Male, female, young, old, football lovers, non-sports fans … they all mourned his loss. Like the deaths of Princess Diana or John Lennon, his was one of those with such intense shock value that you tend to remember where you were and what you were doing on hearing the news.

I was in our Cardiff-based newsroom, having just embarked on what was meant to be a normal busy Sunday shift covering the weekend sport for the following day's newspapers when I received the first call on that terrible morning. This could not possibly be true was my initial reaction – after all, I had seen Speedo just 15 days earlier when his vibrant young Welsh team had hammered a battle-hardened Norway side 4-1 at Cardiff City Stadium. Understandably, he seemed bright and happy enough then as he talked enthusiastically about the future. One which, under Speed, looked as if it was going to be hugely professionally satisfying for the pair of us.

He and I go back a long way, from the first time I talked to him up at Leeds when he was just beginning to make a name for himself as the latest Welsh youngster to break into the top end of the game. At that point, he didn't know me from Adam but instantly agreed to a chat about his hopes and aspirations as a professional footballer. We struck up a rapport. The Gary Speed I talked to back in 1989 was exactly the same man as the one I spoke to every single time afterwards, right up to just before his death. He was charming, polite, amenable and always ready with a good word for others, never a bad one.

On the first occasion we met, he fixed me with that engaging and genuine smile of his and offered a warm handshake. It was to become something of a custom during the intervening years. Even when I wrote things he wasn't entirely comfortable with (invariably, there are occasions in any sports journalism-professional football relationship when criticism must be offered), he never once moped, sulked or held it against me. Occasionally, he might let me know politely what he thought, but having briefly said his piece, he would put things into context for me, invite questions on the next subject we were to talk about and it was business as usual.

When approached to write this book, my initial reaction was one of hesitation: it was too painful, I was a bit too close to the subject matter. However, I quickly realized this project would be a positive rather than a negative. It was to be a celebration of Gary Speed's life rather than an insight into any shadowy matters that may have been troubling him, and if anybody deserved to have a tribute book written about him, that person was Speedo.

He and I shared a common bond, an overriding passion for Welsh football, and together we went through a real roller coaster of a ride: the good, the bad and the occasional downright ugly. Together, we smiled when the Wales team he so splendidly captained famously beat Italy 2-1 at the Millennium Stadium in October 2002. The bars in Cardiff were drunk dry that night. We hurt together when Wales were defeated in win-or-bust qualifiers in Cardiff against Romania (1993) and Russia (2003), in the process destroying hopes of reaching a major finals. We winced together when Wales were embarrassed 7-1 by the Netherlands in Eindhoven in 1997 and 4-0 by Tunisia the following year.

It was Speedo's biggest regret that he never played in the finals of a World Cup or European Championships, something he told me on a number of occasions. Professionally speaking, I responded, mine was that I hadn't had the opportunity to report on Wales playing in a major finals. His chance has come and gone and although I still retain my dream, I can't help thinking it was more likely to happen had he remained at the helm.

Perhaps the greatest thing I have taken from the experience of writing this book is that it has made me realize once again what a very special footballer Gary Speed was. What I mean by this is that many of us (including yours truly) took him a little for granted, simply because of his longevity at the top level of the game. His enormous impact on every team that he played for – Leeds, Everton, Newcastle, Bolton, Wales and even Sheffield United – cannot be overstated.

I myself witnessed so many of those matches. In the early days, he was a rampaging left-winger, whose emergence helped Leeds eclipse Sir Alex Ferguson's Manchester United to win the League title. He then evolved into the prototype of a modern-day midfield man, one who could orchestrate the play, break up opposition moves and control the tempo of a match; he could shoot equally powerfully with either foot, head the ball as well as any centre-half and possessed an athleticism and energy enabling him to cover every single blade of grass on the pitch.

Of course there were others of his era, his great friends Ryan Giggs and Alan Shearer among them, plus the likes of David Beckham, Roy Keane and Thierry Henry, who attracted far more newspaper headlines with their wonderful deeds. However, in his own undemonstrative way, Speedo could be just as influential towards the outcome of a match. A player who could be completely and utterly relied upon by his teammates, often he would seize big games by the scruff of the neck at key moments, sweeping aside the nerves and tension to dominate the midfield with his presence and glide athletically towards the opposition goal to create or score decisive winners. When balls were pumped towards his own goal and needed to be defended, or a brave, last-ditch tackle had to be made with body on the line, we would ask in the press box: 'Who headed that one away?' 'Who blocked that certain goal?' The answer, almost inevitably, was Gary Speed. He would be effective where matches are won and lost, inside the two penalty boxes. For good measure, he also ruled the area of the pitch in between, too.

Invariably, as his Bolton manager, "Big Sam" Allardyce, later points out in this book, Speedo was always there to do it. During a career that saw him play close to 1,000 matches, most of them at the very highest level, he broke all manner of appearance records, goal records and international records. Almost always, he started those games and featured for the full 90 minutes. A mould-breaker in more ways than one, he was the first of the modern Premier League stars to throw his energies into less traditional aspects of football, such as yoga and sports science. Such things might be commonplace among top footballers today, but it was Gary Speed who began the trend.

Typically, each time he broke a record (something that came about fairly frequently once he was in his thirties), he would say: "I will look back upon this proudly one day, but I don't set great stall in personal records. What matters most is the team." He and I used to laugh about what I dubbed his "default setting", but that was Speedo to a T: he always put the team ethic ahead of himself, and he meant it.

Do you know what his finest achievement was, though? That he remained the same level-headed Gary Speed as the one I met all those years ago. Despite fabulous wealth and fame, he never once became too big for his boots, he stayed loyal to his roots and never became embroiled in the type of front-page headlines to have dogged some of his peers. No, Speedo was the squeaky-clean Premier League superstar the public at large could identify with. Which is why, although he played for Leeds, Everton and Newcastle, he was liked and respected by fans of their greatest rivals Manchester United, Liverpool and Sunderland. Not many footballers possess that kind of all-round popularity.

The last time I was in his presence was at that aforementioned Wales friendly international against Norway in Cardiff. Down on the touchline, in his navy FA of Wales blazer complete with matching shirt and tie, he certainly seemed at ease with himself, as he was an hour or so afterwards when holding court with the Welsh media in a room just off the tunnel area at Cardiff City Stadium. He extolled the virtues of his galvanizing young team, spoke excitedly about the future and of how he was travelling to Brussels for a fixtures meeting to arrange the sequence of matches for Wales's looming World Cup campaign.

The following week I tried to get hold of Speedo on his mobile to discuss the outcome of that meeting. There was so much for us to talk about. Was he happy with the order of games? Did he believe that Wales's horrible qualifying jinx could finally be put to bed? It was not uncommon for him not to answer his phone at first, but if you left a message, often he would pick up when you rang back again. On this occasion, sadly, he didn't; I found it strange at the time. I realized the following Sunday morning, when I received the awful first call with the tragic news of his passing, that he had clearly had far more pressing matters on his mind than football.

In the match-day programme for the Wales v. Costa Rica memorial game, held in Gary Speed's honour three months after his death, Alan Shearer wrote: "There has to be a time when you stop asking questions about what happened, because you might never know why. I've tried to do that, but I always come back asking myself 'Why, Speedo?'"

My guess is it's a question that will never go away. Speedo left the football world and a whole nation heartbroken. More importantly, he was the husband, father, brother and son who will most certainly be missed most by those he was closest to. I think it's fair to say that Gary Speed enriched the lives of the many people privileged to have been in his company down the years and though he may be gone, he will never be forgotten.

Paul Abbandonato

1

A Celebration of a Life in Football

Home Team Dressing Room, Cardiff City Stadium, Wales, Wednesday, February 29, 2012: 9.40 p.m.

It was a mild leap-year evening at Cardiff City Stadium and the Wales players had just returned to their dressing room after the most difficult, traumatic and emotionally charged game of football any of them will ever participate in. Exhausted and drained, the distressed teammates sat away from prying eyes, sipping glucose drinks, boots and shin pads strewn everywhere, while waiting for some words of comfort from their stand-in manager for the night, Osian Roberts.

He was the one remaining constant from the senior management side who, for the previous 12 months, had run the Welsh team under the guidance of Gary Speed. One by one, all the others had suddenly departed the scene for various reasons; Speed, of course, in the most tragic circumstances of all. Because he was at least in situ, Roberts, who had been employed as Speed's coach, was placed in sole charge of the side for this one-off memorial match against Costa Rica, which was being held by the Football Association of Wales to honour their former manager. It was the first time the Welsh stars – Gareth Bale, Craig Bellamy and Aaron Ramsey among them – had played together since they had learned of the shock news surrounding their much-loved young manager, barely 13 weeks earlier.

A couple of hours previously, just before they had walked out of the tunnel to play the game, Welsh captain Bellamy had warned his teammates that they were stepping out into the unknown. The atmosphere was going to be different to anything any of them had experienced, or were likely to witness ever again, he explained. He didn't know how he was going to react; they didn't know how they would feel either. What they all had to do, urged Bellamy, in his impassioned pre-match address was to "Go out there and give our best for Gary."

Preparation for the game had been a tearful and distressing experience. Speed wasn't just their manager, but also the players' friend and, in the case of some of the younger stars, their mentor, too. Having to cope without him was an unnerving experience. In the circumstances, it was perhaps inevitable that all the stress and strain the players had gone through would take its toll during the game, which Wales duly lost 1-0.

If Craig Bellamy and the rest of the Welsh team felt they had let down their former manager, any misgivings were instantly swept aside as Roberts, rather than talking to the side himself, brought Speed's eldest son, Edward, into the dressing room. Wearing a red Wales number 11 shirt bearing the name "Speed" on the back, 14-year-old Ed stood in the middle of the players, in the very same spot from which his father had addressed them at the end of their previous match, a Bale-and-Bellamy-inspired 4-1 thrashing of Norway just three months earlier, and promptly delivered the most moving words the players had heard during their careers.

Looking the Welsh stars in the eye, and displaying the most extraordinary confidence and courage in one so young, Speed junior told them: "We've lost tonight, but don't worry too much about it. My dad always said to me that what is important is that you always try your best; as long as you do that's good enough and you all tried your hardest this evening. Thank you for turning up here tonight and playing for my dad."

With that, young Ed went round every single player in the room to warmly shake them all by the hand. He couldn't help but notice tears in the eyes of most of them, which had welled up at the incredibly touching speech they had just been given from such a brave child.

"Ed had already come into the dressing room with his younger brother, Tommy, and Gary's father, Roger, before the Costa Rica match started to wish the players well," recalls stand-in manager, Roberts. "After the game Ed was still in the tunnel area and came up to me to say, 'Os, is it okay if I come in to speak to the players?' 'Of course,' I told him. 'They'll be delighted and privileged to hear what you've got to say.' I brought him in, tried to relax him a little by joking about the colour of his boots (a mix of orange, green and black) and asked the lads to listen up for a moment.

"Ed then delivered his hugely emotional, but perfect speech and the lads had tears in their eyes. We had players in that dressing room who have lost dads or brothers themselves and Ed's speech affected them all in different ways. The one thing everyone was agreed on was how amazing it was that a 14-year-old boy could stand there in front of them, be so mature and give such a brilliant dressing-room talk. I wasn't overly surprised though, because I knew Ed well and how much stronger he was than a lot of even older people, let alone those of a similar age. I later heard he had also spoken just as magnificently to assembled guests upstairs before the match, while he also spoke well at his dad's funeral, which I had attended.

"I can tell you Gary thought so highly of those two boys of his. Not a Wales game went by during his year in charge when he didn't mention them when we were having our meals on our staff table. He and I also went to a lot of games together, so would spend a long time in the car with one another, and invariably Gary mentioned

Tommy's boxing, which he was very much into, or Ed's football, which he was excellent at.

"Gary used to tell me great stories about how he would go home after a Wales match he had just taken charge of, watch the 90 minutes back on video in the front room and Ed would sit there telling him where the team was going right and what they were doing wrong. Ed would say this individual is doing this okay, but that individual is doing that wrong, and inevitably he was right, Gary would explain. For one so young, it was quite remarkable, wasn't it? So, I guess we shouldn't have been too surprised by what happened that night inside our dressing room."

Ed's late father would have been so proud of the manner in which his son addressed those Welsh players, as he would have been a couple of hours earlier when perhaps an even more remarkable and mature show of public speaking was delivered for one so young.

On the third floor at Cardiff City Stadium is the Redrow Suite, a swish hospitality lounge, where invited guests gather before and after matches for food, drink and to talk about the game they are attending. It is the main function room at the state-of-the-art ground, situated a mile down the road from the Millennium Stadium, and which was opened in July 2009 as the new home of Cardiff City FC and Cardiff Blues Rugby Club.

The great and the good of football were inside the Redrow Suite that night, all having travelled to the Welsh capital to pay their respects to a former friend and colleague who meant so much to each and every one of them. Among those present at the Costa Rica game were Speed's former teammates Alan Shearer, Ian Rush and Ryan Giggs, some of his old managers including Howard Wilkinson (Leeds), Mark Hughes and Terry Yorath (both Wales), plus, of course, the family and many friends he had left behind.

The banqueting room was partitioned off into two areas. In one stood Ed, his 13-year-old brother Tom, their mother, Louise, Gary's parents, Roger and Carol Speed, other family members and lots of their friends. In the other were the ex-players, officials and dignitaries.

Roger Gibbins, former Tottenham Hotspur trainee who had two spells as a Cardiff player, is the match-day Master of Ceremonies in the Redrow Suite, where he warmly welcomes guests, gives his professional opinion on the 90 minutes ahead and holds court for any pre-match entertainment. On this occasion, he stood aside and let young Ed take centre stage. Gibbins takes up the tale: "I was told half an hour before kick-off that Louise and the boys wanted to say something, just by way of thanking everybody for their support and for turning up for the game. It was pretty well packed in there, as you can imagine, and I realized we had to find somewhere inside that room where everyone could see the family properly.

"It was very much a spur-of-the-moment thing, so I walked with them over to the entrance to the room, which I thought could be something of a focal point. I pulled a coffee table across, stood up on it so I could have my head above everyone else and asked for people's attention. 'Ladies and gentlemen, we all know this is a very special evening and we have some very special people here, who want to say a few words,' I announced.

"Louise began by thanking everyone for coming to Cardiff that night and for their help and support through the very difficult times, which was lovely. She only spoke briefly, but as you can imagine, every single word was listened to. Then I got up again and said, 'Now we have the second of these very special people who would like to say a few words: Gary's boy, Ed.' He stood on the table so everyone could see him, too, and then proceeded to deliver quite the most remarkable speech I have ever heard in my life.

"Ed talked of how he missed his dad, how his mum's soothing words helped, how she was coping; how his dad had set him and his brother on the right path in life, how his grandfather was so supportive and always drove him to football training and matches of his own. Remember, his dad had died just three months earlier and yet here he was, talking to everyone with such strength, such bottle, such nerve. It wasn't just what he said, it was the way he said it – with composure, a bit of humour when appropriate and supreme confidence. It was a remarkable effort. Ed had some notes in front of him to jog his memory, but only for reminders. Most of it was done so naturally, like ad-libbing.

"There were 400 guests in that room, some real big names from the world of football among them, plus all friends and family. Yet young Ed got up in circumstances you wouldn't wish upon any 14-year-old boy and had us all in tears. He completely set the whole night up for everybody. What was surely a very nerve-racking thing was done by Ed in such a lovely fashion; it was also, in a bizarre sort of way, somewhat reassuring to hear what he had to say – Ed must have been hurting like mad inside, but he was able to deal with the problem in this wonderful way of his. In doing so, it made you think, 'Yes, the family are going to get through this.'

"I can tell you, there were tears in the eyes of pretty much every single person in that room when Ed had finished. He got a rapturous round of applause, which lasted for well over a minute."

Penarth (Cardiff): The Home of Football Association of Wales boss Jonathan Ford, Sunday, November 27, 2011: 9.05 a.m.

The mobile phone rang early in the house of Jonathan Ford, chief executive of the Football Association of Wales. Who on earth could it be at that time of a Sunday morning was his immediate reaction. Reaching across for his handset, he didn't recognize the number calling. Presuming it to be a work-related matter needing his attention, he pressed answer to take the call. The last thing he expected was to hear the voice of Detective Inspector Peter Lawless of Cheshire Constabulary on the other end of the line, let alone what he was about to tell him. The body of a man had been found at a house in Aldford Road, Huntingdon, Chester, the police officer explained, and it was that of Mr Gary Speed.

Naturally, Ford's reaction was one of total disbelief. "It was the most bizarre phone call I have ever had in my life," he recalls. "The police, who are very experienced at handling cases like this, fully understand your state of shock and have a system in place for you to verify the information, which they put into practice. They kept the details very scant, but gave me another telephone number to ring back, in this case the main switchboard at Cheshire Constabulary headquarters, as well as a case number for reference purposes, which I was told to cite.

"I scrambled around for a pen and a piece of paper to write down the number, but in my panicked state of mind I got one of the digits wrong. The number I dialled didn't ring out. I tried to call the police officer back but the line was busy so I left a message, still in a complete daze at what I had only just been told. You can perhaps try to begin to imagine just what I was going through at that particular moment; it was truly horrible. Detective Inspector Lawless texted me back the correct telephone number. I eventually got through [and] gave the case reference, as requested." In hushed tones, he adds: "It was then confirmed for me that Gary had indeed been found dead."

It was three hours earlier, in fact, that Speed's wife, Louise, had discovered the body of her husband, found hanged on the steps leading down to the garage of the luxury £1.5 million Chester home overlooking green fields which they shared with their sons, Edward and Thomas.

The night before, Gary and Louise had been attending a party at a friend's house but after an exchange of words on returning home, Mrs Speed said she was going out for a drive in her car. When she arrived back at the house again, it was locked so she slept in the vehicle, engine running, slipping in and out of fitful sleep. On waking early that fateful Sunday morning, at around 6 a.m., Louise approached the garage, peered through the window and saw her husband on the stairs, his toes in contact with the step. It was at that point when the terrible truth dawned. She woke their two children to open up the house and called the emergency services, but there was nothing they could do to revive her husband. As she hugged her two boys, they in turn tried to comfort her. This was the worst moment of their lives. The shocking news now had to be relayed to other family members, close friends and, of course, Speed's Football Association of Wales (FAW) employers.

Ford, the go-ahead, still relatively new chief executive of the FAW, had grown particularly close to Speed in the preceding 11 months, when in tandem they set about trying to deliver the dream of getting Wales to the finals of a World Cup, something which had not been achieved by the Dragons since 1958. In Speed's homeland, Welsh international football has always had to live in the shadow of Rugby Union, but Ford came into the role having been a lead marketing man with Coca-Cola and was confident about transforming and modernizing the whole set-up. Fundamental to his plans, he decreed, was having Gary Speed as a figurehead for the national team. Marketable, clean-cut and enormously respected, Speed was deemed to be the manager to win over the public at large and get the FAW brand on the bedroom walls of youngsters, a mantra which Ford had set as a goal for everyone within the organization. In the preceding few months the Speed-Ford partnership worked like a dream as Wales won four out of five matches, soared up the FIFA rankings and supporters began showing their greatest interest in the fortunes of the national team for a number of years. Suddenly, because of the impact Speed was making, there was a renewed buoyancy and optimism. Now, in the space of two brief telephone calls, all hope and expectation was shattered.

Somehow Ford needed to put his personal feelings to one side and lead from the front in handling the tragedy in Wales, for this was to be one of the biggest news stories of the year, one that could quickly spiral out of control, too. His first ports of call were FAW media man Ceri Stennett, head of the International Department Mark Evans, FAW President Phil Pritchard and other directors who sat on the governing body. These officials had to hear the news from him first and help him deal with it, rather than learn of the horror already unfolding from TV news bulletins and newspaper websites.

"Getting hold of people on a Sunday morning wasn't the easiest thing in the world to do," says Ford. "Telephones were either off, or people were not answering. For example, I must have rung the President – Phil Pritchard – 10 times before I eventually got through to him. It was a surreal experience, like the whole thing was being played out in slow motion and in something of a daze. I knew a huge story was about to break, but I couldn't get through to all the people I desperately needed to. Eventually, when I did track them down one by one, the reaction from them all was the same as mine had been when the police first rang: shock, disbelief, bewilderment and the inevitable questions of why and how."

By mid-morning, after lots of toing and froing between Cardiff, police liaison in Chester and the Speed family in Huntingdon, Ford had put together an official form of words, which all parties approved. "The police had shown it to Louise and she was okay with the statement, but she still had people to speak to herself to tell them the news so we couldn't release it," he recalls. "There was nothing we could do now, other than to wait for the go-ahead from Louise when she was ready."

It was now shortly before 11 a.m. and having just had the most frantic and distressing two hours of his professional life, Ford decided he needed to clear his head by going for a walk with his family around nearby Cosmeston Lakes, a beauty spot on the outskirts of Cardiff, near to where he lived.

"Just before I walked out of the door, I went over to my computer and did a last-hour Google news search on Gary. Three stories, completely unrelated, came up – none of them, of course, to do with his death," he remembers. "Within five minutes of going for my walk, the police telephoned again on my mobile to say we could release the statement. I instantly rang our media man, Ceri Stennett, to tell him to put it up on the FAW website and to send out emails to our press contacts. Cue bedlam. The website went down within 20 minutes. When I got back from my walk, I pressed the refresh button on my computer. In that short space of time it had gone from three last-hour stories on Gary to more than 100,000. By the end of the week, it was 19.8 million pages.

"I was completely and utterly overcome that day, but somehow you just have to carry on. I have suffered personal loss of my own – my mother and father both dying when they were young. When you lose someone close to you like that, you almost go into some sort of semi-automatic zone and I think that's what I must have done to get through this intense shock."

The official FAW statement was short, sharp and to the point. It read as follows:

We are sad to announce the death of the national team manager Gary Speed. We extend our sympathies and condolences to the family. We ask that everyone respect the family's privacy at this very sad time.

It was now official and so began one of the biggest outpourings of grief this country has ever known following the death of a sporting star or celebrity from any walk of life. Men and women, young and old, football lovers and non-sporting types, fans of Speed's former clubs, supporters of their rivals ... all felt anguish and heartache at the story, which was very quickly leading the major news bulletins and dominated the front five pages of the following morning's national newspapers, as well as the back five.

Some of the front pages kept it simple and to the point, stating in huge type size: "RIP Gary Speed, 8 September 1969 to 27 November 2011".

The *Western Mail*, the respected national newspaper of Wales, devoted its own front page to a picture of Speed in Wales attire accompanied by a short, sharp, two-sentence quote from Aaron Ramsey, the Arsenal starlet whom Speed had made his full-time Welsh captain at the age of just 20 – "I am devastated. The world has lost a great football manager but even more sadly, a great man." No further words were needed. Ramsey's remarks were replicated, inside and outside football, by those who knew Speed and those who didn't but felt as if they did because the former manager was so down-to-earth and likeable. Despite fame and fortune, he was the top football star who never lost his human touch.

At least one national newspaper reported this was not like the deaths of a Nat Lofthouse, Sir Alf Ramsey, Bobby Moore or George Best, who had all lived life to the full. No, this was the sad passing of a man who, at just 42 years of age, was meant to be in the prime of life with everything to look forward to. Instead he had left behind two young boys who doted on their father. In fact, this was one of those rare occurrences in life with such an intense shock value that you tend to remember where you were and who you were with when you first heard the news. Ridiculous though this may sound, other events with a similar resonance were the deaths of John Lennon and Diana, Princess of Wales, in that Paris car crash and the Twin Towers disaster.

As head of sport of Wales's mainstream newspapers, I was in our Cardiff-based newsroom that morning, having just embarked on what was meant to be a normal busy Sunday shift covering the weekend sport for the following day's two daily titles when the first phone call came. Shortly after 10.45 a.m., fellow football writer Terry Phillips uttered the words I will never forget: "Have you heard Gary Speed has been found dead? It's come from a friend who is very close to the family – I think it's true."

Terry's tone was sombre. He knew this was a conversation I did not wish to have. "Don't be so silly," I told him. "That can't be right! Where's that nonsense come from? Can you go back to whoever told you this and find out why this ridiculous rumour has started?"

Terry went away to make the call as requested and, to be honest, I thought little more of what he had just told me; it was simply too preposterous to be true. After all, I had seen Speedo just 15 days earlier – the last time, as it happens – moments after his Wales team had so thrillingly thrashed a battle-hardened Norway 4-1 at Cardiff City Stadium. Certainly, he appeared to be a man at ease with himself that day, smiling, talking positively about what the future held for his side.

Then a second call came from another colleague with the same horrendous message: "Have you heard anything about Gary Speed dying?" Now the rumour was becoming alarming; I didn't like what I was hearing.

In the newspaper industry, we are accustomed to the daftest of rumours starting, gathering absurd momentum and then proving to be, as we had expected from the start, complete and utter nonsense. Sometimes we have to waste time and effort in checking them out, just to be sure. Looking to nip in the bud this particularly wretched piece of gossip, as I presumed it to be, I took the bull by the horns and went straight to the top of the Football Association of Wales. After dialling the telephone number of Phil Pritchard, the FAW President who had appointed Speed to the manager's post less than a year earlier, I started out somewhat hesitatingly: "Phil, I'm sorry to trouble you on a Sunday morning with something as daft as this …" Pausing briefly, almost struggling to say the words, I continued: "But we're hearing horrible things about Gary …" Sadly, the deafening silence at the other end of the line told me all I needed to know. Of course Pritchard had already been given the news by Jonathan Ford. This wasn't scaremongering – tragically, it really was true.

I have been friendly with "Pritch" for more than 20 years. Normally he is a big amiable character, always ready to engage you with a smile and a wisecrack. However, this time there was complete and utter seriousness in his voice. A statement was going to be drawn up by the FAW in Cardiff to be released that lunchtime, he advised. Yes, he knew Gary very well, but no, he hadn't been given any indication of a problem. Nor did he know why it had happened.

No sooner had I put down the receiver than my colleague Terry Phillips called back – "I've rung the family friend again and he says it's definitely true." "Yes, I know," I replied in a daze, scarcely able to think straight. Terry and I both knew Gary and didn't know what more we could say other than Why? How? Where? When?

But we didn't have the answers – it was all guesswork at that stage.

And so began the hardest day of work I have ever had, for emotional reasons more than anything else. In newsrooms, there is a command desk where senior executives regularly sit to discuss the stories of the day and how they are to be presented in terms of word length, headlines and pictures. One of those meetings was taking place as I walked across to interrupt. Everyone looked up at me, but I was open-mouthed for a few seconds, unable to get the words out. Eventually the best I could offer was: "Look, you're not going to believe this but I'm being told Gary Speed has been found hanged."

The execs on the command desk continued to stare at me as if waiting for some sort of punchline but the realization slowly dawned that I would never joke about something as serious as this. What? Why? How? Where? Don't be silly, this isn't really true, is it? The same questions, over and over.

It was a reaction replicated by everybody walking in to begin their shift that day; journalists are a hardened, cynical bunch and precious little shocks those in newsrooms these days. This, however, was the exception to the rule, for no one could quite believe or come to terms with the tragedy now unfolding. Gary Speed was one of our own in Wales – this could not be happening. Extra staff were called in and the page planning taking place was ripped up; that day in the office some of us got by on gut instinct alone.

Very quickly a flood of glowing tributes began pouring in, not just from leading football figures but also from lots of people who didn't even know Speed. The accolades came from the worlds of pop music, showbiz, even Parliament, but mostly there were messages of condolence for the family from Joe Public on Facebook, Twitter and various Internet football messageboard websites. Via a mix of official statements, interviews with the media and social networking, this is a small selection of what was said:

RYAN GIGGS (former Wales teammate of Speed):
"I am totally devastated. Gary Speed was one of the nicest men in football and someone I am honoured to call a teammate and friend. It goes without saying my thoughts are with his family at this tremendously sad time."

ALAN SHEARER (former Newcastle United teammate and friend):
"Gary was a magnificent person, bright, fun and a wonderful family man. He lit up every room he walked into. I am proud to have been his friend and will miss him dreadfully."

ROBBIE SAVAGE (another former Wales teammate):
"The world has lost a great man. I'm devastated – spoke to him yesterday morning. Why, why, why? I will miss him so much. He came to watch *Strictly Come Dancing*, three to four weeks ago; I high-fived him in the front row. He loved the show, he loved life, he loved his family … Devastated."

RICHARD SCUDAMORE (Premier League chief executive):
"Gary will go down in history as one of our iconic players. He was a stand-out professional of the modern game and I'm sure all football fans across Britain will be deeply saddened at his untimely passing."

KENNY DALGLISH (Speed's former Newcastle United manager):
"He was a very respected man in and around football, not only for his ability but for the guy as a person."

AARON RAMSEY (Wales captain):

"I was given the tragic news this morning. To say I am devastated is an understatement. My thoughts and prayers go out to Gary's family and friends. Today the world has lost a great football manager but even more sadly a great man. He will be missed by all."

ROBIN VAN PERSIE (Arsenal striker):

"I heard the sad news about Gary Speed. Great footballer, my condolences and sympathies to his family."

JOE ROYLE (former Everton manager):

"He always had a smile on his face, he played with a smile on his face and he was one of the best players I was fortunate enough to manage and handle and I still can't believe it."

MICHAEL OWEN (former England striker and neighbour):

"Just cannot believe the news regarding Gary Speed. We waved at each other a couple of days ago, dropping our kids off at school. I'm numb."

HOWARD WILKINSON (Speed's former Leeds United manager):

"It's such a loss. I cannot begin to try to understand what his parents are thinking. I knew his mum and dad, and particularly his dad very well. I've met a lot of people in my time, a lot of sportsmen. Gary had none of those things which we associate with sportsmen: he was ordinary as a bloke, very nice, very genuine, very honest; very hard-working. He was a joy to manage."

XABI ALONSO (Spain and Real Madrid midfielder):
"RIP Gary Speed. My first Premier League game was against him – he showed me in that game what British football is about."

GARY NEVILLE (former Manchester United player):
"It's absolutely devastating. My career and his crossed many times; I played against him many times. Everyone I know who knew him couldn't say enough good things about him. We think of football as being important, but it's not really."

DAVID BECKHAM (former England opposing captain):
"He was an amazing, talented player, a player that had such a glittering career and had just began a great career in management as well. We'd like to send our love and thoughts to his wife, his children and family. It is a sad time to lose a man like this."

SEPP BLATTER (FIFA President):
"I would like to offer my deepest condolences on behalf of FIFA and the worldwide family of football to you, the Football Association of Wales, his wife, Louise, and their two sons, as well as Gary Speed's friends and family. I hope the knowledge that we are all thinking of them can provide some solace in this time of deep sadness. He will always be remembered as a model professional and a fantastic ambassador for the game. He was a man who exuded enthusiasm and passion for the game."

NIALL QUINN (former Sunderland striker):
"His career speaks for itself but the esteem in which he was held universally was immense and absolutely unique."

As the tributes flowed in, many of those who had got to know Speed well through football somehow had to prepare themselves for Premier League matches scheduled to take place that very afternoon. One such fixture involved Swansea City, who were playing Aston Villa at the Liberty Stadium in Wales. Three of the Swansea players – defenders Ashley Williams and Neil Taylor, plus midfielder Joe Allen – had become key players in Speed's Wales set-up and inevitably found the occasion extremely upsetting, as did the Aston Villa goalkeeper that day, Shay Given, who was one of Speed's best friends, having played next to him up at Newcastle for many years. The tears the Republic of Ireland goalkeeper shed in public at kick-off time, captured on TV images and widely displayed in the following day's newspapers, underlined everything he thought of the news he had just learned. Given, Speed and Alan Shearer had regularly played golf together on Tyneside and were family friends as well as football colleagues.

In due course Given and Shearer would help carry Speed's coffin into the church for the private funeral, held near to where he grew up in Hawarden, north Wales. Another pallbearer was Craig Bellamy, who had played with Speed at Newcastle and would regularly travel down to Cardiff with his friend for international duty with Wales. Bellamy, too, was scheduled to play on that Sunday afternoon – for Liverpool against Premier League title winners to be, Manchester City, at Anfield – but was too distressed to go through with the match. At the eleventh hour manager Kenny Dalglish pulled him from the side, granting him compassionate leave to grieve privately.

The following morning FAW chief executive Jonathan Ford, still reeling at the news he had received 24 hours earlier from Detective Inspector Peter Lawless, had to gather his staff together at the governing body's purpose-built headquarters in the Cardiff Bay area of the Welsh capital. One by one, those employees had gone in to work in something of a trance, scarcely able to believe they would never again see the man they so greatly respected and whom they regarded as a friend, and not just the manager of their country.

"That impromptu staff meeting we held in the offices was the most harrowing moment for me," says Ford. "By that stage I had noted how every morning newspaper had devoted not just the back pages to the story, but also the front pages too. We all knew just how big this was, but to us this was about Gary, our colleague.

"With the President, Phil Pritchard, standing right by my side, I went through with the staff what I had been doing over the previous 24 hours. It was a very emotional meeting as we talked about what we needed to do next, how we had to be strong and get through this together; how we were going to open a condolence book of remembrance. All of us inside that room had grown very fond of Gary. He wasn't just the national team manager, he was also the mate who, when we went to the pub on a Friday night after work, would come along with us, put his debit card behind the bar and buy everybody drinks. We cried together that day and when we had finished talking, we stood there in the room for a minute's silence, paying our own respects to Gary in private."

For Ford and Pritchard, the duties were far from over. After briefing the FAW staff, they were then obliged to go out and talk to the media at a hastily convened press conference held at St David's Hotel, overlooking the Bristol Channel. Less than a year earlier, Ford and Pritchard had sat either side of Speed to proudly announce him as their new manager. On that occasion, the company logos of the FAW's main business partners were on display, as is the norm at such media gatherings. This time there could be no such backdrop: Ford and Pritchard had to speak as friends of Gary, rather than as chief executive and president of the Football Association of Wales. They displayed commendable patience in ensuring they did not turn down a single request for an interview that day, whether for TV, radio or print journalism. As expected, a mass of media was present for what was such a huge story. The two FAW bosses acted with dignity and spoke magnificently in extremely trying circumstances.

While that was going on, the Speed family members were grieving in private and Gary's agent and close friend Hayden Evans had to meet the press on their behalf to read out a prepared statement, thanking the public for the words of support and comfort they had been offering over the past 24 hours. It was perhaps the most difficult thing Evans had ever done in his life because for him Speed was far more than just a client on his books. He had represented Speed throughout his career, having set up his own football consultancy firm at the end of the 1980s. Very quickly, the two men built up a bond, so much so that Evans asked Speed to act as best man at his wedding.

Of that particular Monday morning, he recalls: "The police had asked us to read out a statement outside the family home in north Wales to disperse the waiting media who had all gathered. Clearly none of the family members were in any sort of state to be able to do it, so the responsibility inevitably fell to me. It was the last thing I wanted to do, but I knew I just had to grin and bear it and get on with it. I was in front of TV cameras and the written media, and I only just about managed to hold myself together. As I read out the words, I could notice myself choking up inside. It was a very painful experience for me, something I knew I had to do for the sake of the family.

"Even more horrible, of course, was learning the tragic news the day before. Every Sunday I go to watch my son James play football for his local side in Leeds. My mobile telephone is often glued to my ear, but on this occasion I unwittingly had left it at home, probably for the first time ever. As I went into the clubhouse that lunchtime,

I was in a reasonably jolly mood. We had won the game, James had played well, and we were chatting away when a strapline about Gary's death suddenly appeared on the TV in the clubhouse.

"It was my son who brought it to my attention. 'Is that about our Gary?' he asked me, pointing to the TV screen. I looked up, saw the words, couldn't begin to comprehend the news, picked James up, got back in the car and dashed home. I retrieved my mobile from the house and noticed I had 12 missed calls from Gary's out-and-out best mate, John Ratcliffe, who he knew from north Wales. His voicemail message told me what had happened. It was really difficult for me that Sunday afternoon because I was looking after James and his twin sister Hannah and somehow had to try to remain strong in front of them. In private though, when I got a moment to myself, I broke down in tears.

"Then it was a case of dashing over to Huntington to be with the family. Lots of people were already there, trying to comfort one another. 'Why?', was the question we all asked. There had not even been an inkling of a problem with Gary. On the contrary, he was talking about meeting up with people, planning for the future. Like everyone else, I couldn't begin to get my head around what had happened."

In other parts of Britain, the tributes continued to pour in. Wreaths, scarves, shirts and flowers were laid outside the grounds of Leeds, Everton, Newcastle, Bolton and Sheffield United – the clubs Speed so splendidly represented during the course of his 22-year playing career. Something similar happened outside his Cheshire house, one poignant message simply reading: "*Nos Da*" (Welsh for "Goodnight").

Such was the shock of Speed's passing, it was inevitable questions would be asked as to why such a leading football figure – a man who appeared to have everything going for him in terms of good looks, fame, fortune and a job as manager of Wales which he adored – would supposedly take his own life. Did he do so deliberately, or was it an accident? The speculation was bound to increase, particularly as this was one of the first high-profile deaths of the new social networking era and everyone, it seemed, wanted to have their say on what they thought might be the reason, although the level and content of some of the conjecture certainly shocked one or two members of the Speed family. Gary's own brother-in-law, Anthony Haylock, who is married to his sister, Lesley, would later take to Twitter himself to publicly slam some of the more scurrilous rumour-mongering.

Away from the Internet gossip, much was made of a TV appearance given by Speed on BBC's *Football Focus* show the day before his death. His friend Alan Shearer was in the studios that lunchtime, laughing and joking with him, and they were due to talk again on the Monday morning to arrange a round of golf. Speed, we were assured by those involved in the production, looked his normal, amiable, happy self.

Some of us begged to differ, though. On looking back at the programme in our Media Wales offices the following afternoon, we felt he looked white in the face and something – and I couldn't quite put my finger on what it was – just didn't seem right. It's easy to be wise in hindsight, but it's almost as if he was forcing a smile. It certainly wasn't the natural beaming Speed grin to which I had become accustomed in my dealings with him down the years. Interestingly, Speed's mother and father each made similar assertions in due course. At her son's inquest, Carol Speed said of that TV appearance: "Gary was smiling – but it did not reach his eyes."

Gary's father, Roger, in an interview given for Sky TV ahead of the Costa Rica memorial match, said he too realized all was not right on seeing the video of the *Football Focus* programme again. "Looking at it a few times, I could see there was something troubling him," he said.

Quite what that was never became clear, even when the full inquest was heard in Warrington, two months after Speed's death, as Cheshire coroner Nicholas Rheinberg recorded a narrative verdict. He could not be satisfied, he adjudged, that Gary Speed had intended to kill himself.

Speed's widow, Louise, spoke publicly for the first time of how she discovered her husband's body hanging at their home, of how there was a strain on their marriage – although this was something all couples experienced at times – and how she and her husband had had words when they returned from a dinner party the night before. Four days earlier, she revealed, Gary had sent her a text talking "in terms of taking his life", but she said he had then dismissed it because of their children. The text conversation referred to their "ups and downs" but also mentioned "how important the boys were" and about "moving forward".

She told the inquest: "The texts went on about our future together and how excited he was about our journey together." Speaking in hushed tones, Louise described her husband as "quite a closed character – he looked to take on board everyone else's problems. He wouldn't be a person to open up himself: he was very private. Like all couples, we would be going through ups and downs in our marriage and we were working through it."

Also giving evidence, Speed's mother, Carol, described her son as a man of few words. "He was always a glass-half-empty person, certainly no optimist. I don't know why he didn't talk to us if there was something making him unhappy. He was so popular, there would always have been someone there to talk to," she said. The phone call from her daughter-in-law that fateful morning, she added, was the "worst moment of my life."

The inquest was told by the Welsh national team's GP, Dr Mark Ridgewell, that Speed had shown no signs of stress or depression, a view echoed by his counterpart at Sheffield United – the last club he had been with before becoming manager of his country.

Recording his narrative verdict, Mr Rheinberg said: "It seems likely that Mr Speed was sitting for some time with a ligature around his neck. It may have been that this was some sort of dramatic gesture, not normally in Mr Speed's character, but nonetheless a possibility." He said Speed may have "nodded off to sleep" with the ligature still around his neck.

Following the verdict, the Speed family issued a statement in which they said:

Gary's death, and the manner of it, made Sunday 27th November 2011 the worst day of our lives. Throughout the nine weeks since, there have been some very dark moments, which we have all had to find our own different ways to endure.

Now, we have to adapt to the future without a husband, a father, a brother and a son; but Gary's memory shines brightly in our thoughts and we will forever remember the wonderful times we shared with him and the deep love and affection he offered so freely within our close-knit family.

Thankfully, out of tragedy some good often emerges, and we feel blessed to have such true friends who are helping each of us come to terms with the circumstances of our bereavement.

Gary's funeral was an occasion of great sadness and grief for everyone concerned but it was also a day where we were able to say farewell to him in our own personal and private way.

At this time we wish to reiterate our deep appreciation for the very generous and clearly sincere accolades paid to Gary and his memory by the public and all forms of the media.

Louise, her children and Speed's parents had gone through some very public mourning ahead of the inquest. A week after his death, they travelled to Elland Road, Speed's spiritual football home, for the Leeds v. Millwall Championship match, where they were joined by his former midfield teammates Gordon Strachan, David Batty and Gary McAllister in laying wreaths on the pitch he once used to grace so magnificently in helping the club secure the League title at the beginning of the 1990s. Louise was then taken to the statue of Billy Bremner, just outside the ground, to see the flowers, scarves and shirts that had been left and to read the many personal messages of support and condolence from Leeds fans.

A couple of weeks later, the family attended the Newcastle v. Swansea Premier League game, linking arms in the centre circle before kick-off as the sell-out Toon Army who adored Speed so much paid their respects to the man who wore the black-and-white number 11 shirt for seven years.

Gary's father, Roger, said in an interview with Sky TV: "People have been wonderful – I didn't realize how many friends we had. The response has been unbelievable. We've had letters and cards from people we don't even know. They just put down our name and the mail has arrived. We've had letters from all over the world – Australia, New Zealand, Canada … People have been so kind, it's given us such a lift."

The final occasion of public mourning was the Wales v. Costa Rica memorial match in Cardiff, which went off so well the FA of Wales were commended for their handling of the occasion and received letters of thanks from the Speed family.

"I had deliberately stayed away from the funeral," explains chief executive Jonathan Ford. "I was Gary's employer who had known him, albeit very well, for just a year. His family and friends had known him all his life and they had to be left alone to grieve in their own way. Obviously, we helped out in any way we could. For example, Gary's parents, Roger and Carol, and sister, Lesley, wanted to come down to Cardiff to have a look around his office and the flat he stayed in when working down here, so we accommodated that request. I took them to the flat, which overlooks the Bristol Channel. They turned to me and said, 'Yes, we can imagine our Gary enjoying it here. This is the sort of view he would have liked.' They also said he loved the Wales job so much. What I knew we had to do as Gary's former employers was to ensure the Costa Rica match was an occasion which did justice to his memory and which we could all be proud of, including his family."

On that score, the FAW received full marks. February 29, 2012 at Cardiff City Stadium was indeed an inspiring and heartening evening as the Welsh public bade farewell to the manager who had given them such hope and optimism for a brief period that their national team was, at last, ready to wow the football world. A record crowd of 23,193 filled the ground for an occasion that somewhat bizarrely, given that this was a memorial match, had more of a carnival-type feel to it than any sense of sombreness. Beforehand tenor Bryn Terfel and a massed male voice choir gave a splendid rendition of "Bread of Heaven" as videos of Speed's finest moments, both as a Wales player and as a manager, were displayed on the big screen to rapturous applause.

Mike Peters of Welsh rock band The Alarm then sang "You're Just Too Good To Be True, Can't Take My Eyes Off You" – the Andy Williams hit that Speed so adored and which had become something of a theme tune for the Welsh team he once starred in. It had also been played at both his wedding and his funeral, with Kelly Jones of the Stereophonics penning his own version in Speed's honour.

The emotion of the occasion really hit home, though, when Speed's sons, Ed and Tom, led the Wales team out of the tunnel, each wearing red shirts bearing the name of their father, one with number 11 on the back, the other with number six. Holding hands with Craig Bellamy (captain for the evening in the absence of the injured Aaron Ramsey), they walked onto the pitch for the playing of the national anthems. I have attended all the major Welsh sporting events of recent times, including three Grand Slam-winning rugby matches (2005, 2008 and 2012) in front of capacity 74,500 crowds at the Millennium Stadium, but never before have I heard "*Mae Hen Wlad Fy Nhadau*" (Land of My Fathers) sung with such emotion and gusto as it was that night at Cardiff City Stadium. Leading the way were young Ed and Tom, Bellamy at the centre of them, his arms embracing each for comfort. Their father used to love singing that anthem before Wales matches, both as a player and then as a manager, and now his sons were following in his footsteps.

With Bellamy continuing to keep a close eye on them, the Speed boys helped exchange pennants with the Costa Rica captain and then walked off to resounding applause from the Welsh fans. On the halfway line at the side of the pitch, where their dad once stood for games, there with his arms open wide and ready for a big embrace was their grandfather Roger. It was incredibly touching.

There was meant to be a minute's applause in celebration of Speed's life before kick-off. However, the standing ovation began long before World Cup Final referee Howard Webb, the man in the middle, blew his whistle. The applause went on and on and on … and then on and on, and on again. It lasted a full three minutes and the noise was so loud, it was impossible to hear the shrill of Webb's whistle as he blew for it to cease. It only happened because the players broke away from the semicircle where they had lined up together in Speed's honour, knowing there was a game of football to be played.

Wales fell behind to a Joel Campbell goal early on, but during those 90 minutes the Welsh supporters chanted the name of their former manager pretty much throughout. Never before at a football game has one man commanded so much of a non-stop ovation: it was very much a celebration of Speed's life, rather than a wake.

The Welsh fans regularly broke into their own version of their hero's favourite song, "Can't Take My Eyes Off You". They also chanted "Gary Speed's Barmy Army", "There's Only One Gary Speed" and "Stand Up If You Love Speedo". First up from their seats for that final chant, down by the touchline watching the match with their grandfather, were Edward and Thomas Speed, quickly followed by an entire stadium.

For Osian Roberts, stand-in manager for the evening, those 90 minutes of football were perhaps the easiest part, even though he had never before taken charge of a team at anything remotely resembling this level. His most pressing issue had been beforehand in trying to comfort his players, who were coming into camp for the first time without the manager they had so grown to admire. Roberts wanted to ensure everything done in the build-up to the game was fitting for Speed's legacy and that he would be given a send-off to make his family feel special. Like Jonathan Ford, he delivered his part of the bargain, but it wasn't easy because he was pretty much on his own as the match approached.

When Speed was at the helm, Roberts had formed part of a four-man backroom team of lieutenants who met regularly with the manager to plan the way forward with Wales. The others making up this five-pronged management set-up were Speed's number two, Raymond Verheijen, an outspoken but influential Dutchman who helped shape strategy, operations manager Adrian Davies and sports science expert Damian Roden. One by one, for entirely differing reasons, they were gone by the time the Costa Rica game came around, leaving Roberts the last man standing.

"There was no coaching manual I could look at to tell me what to do in these circumstances. It all had to be on the hoof, almost from the heart as much as from the head," recalls Roberts. "We had been in limbo for a while. For a long period of time we hadn't been able to think about the football, only of Gary's death, but as the days drew on, and I was told I would be in charge for this memorial match, I knew I just couldn't let down Gary or his family: we had to provide a fitting tribute to his legacy.

"A lot of time was spent on looking after the players' well-being. How did we do that? we wondered at first. They were coming back into the team hotel for the first time since our win over Norway and there would be a staff table in the room with a seat empty on it. Everyone would handle the situation differently; we just had to be as supportive and sympathetic as we could. Some players didn't want to talk about Gary; others wanted to go through the process by discussing what had happened. We had to do all this before we began to even think of the 90 minutes of football ahead.

"Once we were all in camp, I brought the players into a room at our hotel base for a meeting. No chairs, not a question of 'I'm speaking to you' or anything like that. We gathered together, I stood in the middle, looked around and told them there was no science that could tell me how to handle this moment; it was gut instinct. I talked about the sad occurrence and how it was important to go through with this tribute match for Gary.

"The one thing we all did know was that Gary would have wanted us to play the game and continue our development as a team building towards the World Cup qualification campaign starting that autumn. This game was part of the mission to get us to the end of the vision, another building block towards Brazil 2014 and further tournaments beyond that. 'Gary would not have wanted us to stand still,' I explained. 'Certain things are no longer as they were but we have to remain strong for each other.'

"We asked the players for their input. It was a difficult time – by and large they were quiet and sombre. Some spoke, others didn't, but it was important we had that time together. Then we put a two-minute video of Gary, the team and his staff on the screen. We had spent an awful lot of time and energy putting this video together; every single clip had to be the right one – we dared not get a single second wrong. I simply told the players, 'This is something to remember him by.' At that point we hugged each other, linked arms and stood there to watch the screen. Some of the players were tearful, but we had to go through that process. The moment the video finished, you could see how choked the players were. Yes, there were tears in their eyes.

"Then we went out for a walk together, the sort of thing Gary liked to do when we gathered in camp as part of a team-bonding exercise – he always used to be out in the front. He would have wanted us to carry that on, so we did. I also told the players there was a Sky TV camera in the next room and they could go in and pay their respects to Gary, if they so wished. The comments would then be broadcast just ahead of the game on the Wednesday evening. There was no gun to anybody's head, it was all voluntary. Some did it; others said, 'Os, I can't do this. I will break down in tears if I go in there and start speaking.' So they didn't do it – there was no pressure put on.

"It was against this backdrop that we had to play the game itself and, to be honest, I knew we would have a bad start, be somewhat off the pace. I also knew there was probably nothing I could have done about it. We conceded a goal after just seven minutes and at half-time, as they trooped in and sat down, I could see the players were drained. I spoke to one or two and they said, 'Os, I don't know what it is, but I can't move my legs.'

"We're talking here about big-name footballers who were playing every minute of every game for their Premier League clubs. It was at that point I realized all the emotion of the week had taken its toll on them physically, too. The last thing I needed to do was talk tactics, or anything like that – this was only about the boys giving their best in the most difficult of circumstances."

Try as they might in the second half, roared on by the Welsh fans willing a goal in Gary Speed's name, those players simply could not turn around the 1-0 half-time deficit. However, they still walked off to a standing ovation at the end and if any of them felt they had let down Gary's memory, they were quickly put right in the privacy of the dressing room, as young Ed addressed them with that courageous speech of his. It was perhaps significant that Speed junior made those players feel so much better about themselves with his moving words. Why? Because the way in which he and his younger brother, Tom, behaved so bravely that evening in Cardiff perhaps exemplified the way their father had played out his own football career.

Strong, respected, always leading by example, always trying to help others on the pitch and in the dressing room ... that was Gary Speed for you. The strength of character personifying his playing career will emerge time and again in the coming chapters in celebration of a very special footballer. He had so much going for him, which is why family, friends and fans still today ask one question: why, Gary?

2

A Player Ahead of His Time

"I've always been prepared to embrace new ideas."

Gary Speed

Gary Speed was a special and unique footballer. On the field of play he broke records galore, setting a whole string of football firsts in over 20 years. Off the field, he avoided controversy and was prepared to experiment with what were then revolutionary new ideas in a bid to improve his game, such as taking weekly yoga classes and even having ball-kicking lessons, well into his mid-thirties.

Away from the training ground and the football, Speed was also the Premier League player who throughout his illustrious career remained very much in tune with the people. He was the man with the common touch, the football star that the paying public always liked, respected and could identify with. It didn't matter if they were a supporter of one of the teams Speed played for or a fan of one of his big rivals, there was something very modest about him that endeared him to the public and that was almost certainly the reason why there was such an outpouring of grief at the news of his death in November 2011.

Rightly or wrongly, it is fair to say that footballers have not always enjoyed a good press down the years, with high-profile players capturing the wrong sort of headlines for a variety of reasons. Up until his shocking death, Speed had never attracted bad publicity for himself, his family, his employers or his profession. As a player and manager, he always retained a touch of dignity and was liked by all.

Because he didn't fly down the wing like Ryan Giggs, score the goals of Alan Shearer, or set the fashion and drive home free kicks as splendidly as David Beckham, Speed did not stand out as prominently as others from his era. Good old reliable Gary was the way he was perceived. What he achieved on an individual basis, however, eclipsed more than virtually every single one of his peers and marked him down as a genuine football great.

When he was with Bolton, Speed became the first footballer to make 500 appearances in the Premier League. His record tally of 535 games – played for Leeds, Everton, Newcastle and Bolton – was only beaten when former England goalkeeper David James made it 536 matches for himself in February 2009, on appearing for Portsmouth against Manchester City. James's own record of 573 Premier League matches was subsequently overtaken two years later when Ryan Giggs made it 574 games for Manchester United, playing in a title-clinching 1-1 draw at Blackburn. It is hard to envisage anyone, certainly in the near future, eclipsing Giggs.

When he headed a goal for Bolton against Reading on August 25, 2007, Speed became the only player to score in every single season since the inception of the Premier League in 1992–93. Only Giggs was able to first match and then better that feat, scoring for Manchester United in a 1-0 win at West Ham in February 2009. At international level, Speed became Wales's record cap holder for an outfield player, appearing 85 times for his country; he captained the Dragons a record 44 times and possessed the best wins per game ratio (50 per cent, five victories from 10 matches) of any manager in the country's history.

For a full two decades, Speed played at the top level, appearing in a staggering 926 matches in total. He had one early season in the old Division Two with Leeds, back in 1989–90, when they won the title and promotion to the top flight and a brief spell in the Championship with Sheffield United right at the end of his playing days. Other than that, every other game with club or country was at the top end.

To put Speed's total of 926 matches into some sort of perspective, perhaps I should cite the case of AC Milan and Italian legend Paolo Maldini, who is always held up as the doyen of world football when it comes to longevity at the highest level. Over the course of a career spanning from 1985 to 2009 (three years more than Speed), Maldini appeared in 1,028 games. Exactly 902 of them were for AC Milan, the other 126 in the blue of the Azzurri. Maldini was quite rightly revered as a genuine icon of the world game and his achievements stretching over 24 years were nothing short of staggering.

Nor, when we examine them, though, were those of Speed, who played 841 club matches and 85 times for Wales, making up the 926 tally. Okay, 80 of those club games were in the second tier of English football whereas Maldini was always at the forefront of the Italian game, winning Serie A titles and UEFA Champions Leagues. That said, Maldini first played left-back and then centre-half. One of the greatest we have ever seen, it has to be stressed, but nonetheless a defender who never had to cope with the demands that went with being a more attacking-orientated player such as Speed. Maldini could sit in the back four during some matches and take a breather, particularly in a team as dominant as AC Milan, who possessed true world-class match-winners further forward, such world stars as Ruud Gullit, Marco van Basten, George Weah and Brazilian great Kaka. Speed, in the midfield engine room, had to be right in the thick of it all for every single minute of every single game – up, down, back, forth, scoring the goals, stopping the goals, creating them, putting in last-ditch tackles.

The record books show that Speed scored 142 times during his career, an impressive statistic in its own right for a midfield player. What they don't display of course is how many goals he created for his teammates or stopped with defensive efforts, energy, athleticism and willingness to help out his defence.

Ryan Giggs went on to overtake Speed's British appearances record. His 900th game for Manchester United came in a Premier League fixture against Newcastle in February 2012 and Giggs could also throw another 64 internationals for Wales into the mix. Once more, it is hard to imagine anyone coming close to eclipsing those feats. However, Giggs's supreme efforts should not take anything away from Gary Speed's own record-breaking achievements because he was the first Briton of the modern age to demonstrate that sort of longevity. In the past, a number of other lower-division players have held appearance records and were rightly lauded for so doing. John Trollope of Swindon Town played 770 games for one club between 1960 and 1980. Overall, Terry Paine (of Southampton, Hereford and England) made 824 appearances in the 1950s, 60s and 70s before Tony Ford (who played for teams such as Grimsby, Sunderland, Scunthorpe, Mansfield and Rochdale) usurped him, going into the record books with 931 games.

Each of these individuals is afforded legendary status in their particular corner of Britain because of their deeds but first Speed and then Giggs took matters to a whole new level. They survived the test of time in the modern era's most demanding League when players needed to be a lot fitter because football became a much faster game. One of the reasons for this was the outlawing of the backpass rule, which meant the ball-in-play time was greater and there was no opportunity to slow the tempo by letting your goalkeeper pick up the ball, bounce it a few times and give everyone a much-needed breather. That Speed survived in, and thrived, on the hurly-burly nature of the modern game, being picked to star in almost every single one of those 926 matches and playing the full 90 minutes in most of them, was testament not only to his natural fitness but also to his willingness to embrace new ideas.

These days, sports science is the norm at top football clubs but when Gary Speed first broke into the game at the tail end of the 1980s, that sort of off-the-field preparation was viewed as rare, radical and revolutionary and was pretty much scorned by the cynics. Speed's Leeds United mentor Howard Wilkinson, himself a visionary, introduced his protégé to the quieter arts, explaining how the game of football wasn't just about 90 minutes on a Saturday afternoon but the whole build-up as well. The young Speed was instantly bitten by the sports science bug and became a huge backer of the high-tech approach over the next 20-plus years, often leading the way as he looked for an extra edge.

For a year the Wales team he managed were possibly as forward thinking about training and international games as any other side in world football. Among his backroom staff, Speed armed himself with leaders in their chosen fields, whether nutrition, video analysis or medics, giving daily saliva and blood tests to Gareth Bale and his colleagues and analysing the results to determine just how fit they were.

Speed's conviction about what others may consider gimmicks all started at Leeds when he saw a 34-year-old Gordon Strachan defy age and appear alert and ready to go every single time he took to the field of play. Naturally he asked him the secret of his success. "Eating bananas and seaweed," came back the answer. Throw in some good old-fashioned Welsh cawl (meat and potato soup), lots and lots of vitamin supplements and special drinks for rehydration and Speed had a diet that he would follow for the remainder of his football career.

"The impact Gordon had on me was absolutely tremendous," he readily admitted, when asked towards the latter part of his career for the secrets of his record-breaking longevity. "He was so fit and a living example for me of how I should behave, on and off the pitch, in order to get as much as I could out of the game. Gordon was a firm believer in eating and drinking the right foods and this was at a time, remember, when footballers believed they could eat what they wanted. Obviously, as time moved on, players realized that wasn't the case, but Gordon was way ahead of his time.

"When I was a young player with Leeds, I would watch Gordon with his bananas and seaweed cakes and wonder what the heck he was eating that for. In those days, if I was hungry I used to just stop off at Burger King. Then Gordon would suddenly race past me in training and I would realize he was right and I was wrong. I took on board a lot of the advice he gave me and it proved to be invaluable.

"Gordon was doing things in the early 1990s that people just started doing in the next millennium. I was fortunate enough to play alongside him and see how someone in the latter stages of his career looked after himself. I was clever enough to watch him and take it on board. He won the Footballer of the Year award when he was 34, which says everything, really. He used to dominate games from the right wing and that's a very difficult thing to do. He was unbelievable."

There can be little doubt that the diet carefully planned from an early age helped Speed survive the test of time as he went on to usurp even Strachan, but he was also prepared to go that extra mile in other spheres in order to remain at the top. When he was with Bolton, for example, Speed revealed that he had decided to take up the ancient art of yoga. In the macho world of football that would have raised an eyebrow (or three) at the time, but he himself did not bat an eyelid.

"I do it twice a week at home, with a personal teacher. At my age in my thirties, it is a great exercise for suppleness," he explained, and went on to describe how yoga helped with his athleticism, strength and energy and reduced stress levels, all designed to squeeze extra mileage out of what was by now an ageing body, at least in football terms.

"I've always been prepared to embrace new ideas, but as you get older, you realize you need an edge to keep up with the younger players coming through," he continued. "I was there at the beginning of the Premier League and the changes since it began are breathtaking. The game of football is the same but everything else has moved on and the biggest difference is the level of fitness and athleticism. Injury prevention is important and that's why I have been having yoga classes twice a week for the last three years. Once upon a time everybody would have laughed at that, but it has stopped me having the back problems that, historically, have troubled older players."

Once he had embarked on yoga, others began to follow suit. They could see that what was good for Speed, given the way he continued to perform so superbly at the top level well into his late thirties, could be good for them, too. However, Speed didn't stop there. Another revolutionary idea that he took on board while at Bolton was to have kick-the-ball lessons from rugby union expert Dave Alred. Now the thought of someone of Speed's age, by then well into his mid-thirties, wanting to learn how to boot a ball properly after he had already broken all manner of football records and scored countless goals again raised eyebrows at the time. However, he had noted how Jonny Wilkinson struck a rugby ball so beautifully in guiding England to their 2003 Rugby World Cup triumph in Sydney, Australia, when Sir Clive Woodward's England beat the host nation in a thrilling final. Wilkinson put much of his success down to the tricks of the trade passed on by his kicking mentor Alred, also a personal tutor of the Wales kicking great, Neil Jenkins.

Not a bad duo then when it came to references and always willing to embrace new ideas. Speed thought that he too could gain an extra edge from working with Alred and so, at 35 years of age, he was a willing participant when the then Bolton manager, Sam Allardyce (another sports science enthusiast), asked Alred to visit the club's training headquarters at the Reebok Stadium to show his players a thing or two when it came to how best to strike a ball.

Following the training session, Speed couldn't praise Alred enough, saying openly: "While footballers can be a cynical lot, I found his work with me really enlightening and thoroughly enjoyed it. Basically, Dave was asked to come in and help us with our shooting. He gave me a few things to practise when I strike the ball – what to do in order to gain extra power and accuracy and exactly what part of the ball I should be aiming to hit. With practice, the idea is for me to repeat this instinctively amid the intensity of a game. These new ideas – doing yoga, cutting out junk food and only drinking in moderation – are important factors in keeping me going strong at my age."

The only player able to rival Speed for longevity, grabbing even greater success at the top level, was fellow countryman Ryan Giggs. Together, the two lined up in the red of their country more than 60 times and Speed could always see the similarities between them as men who thrived on playing and winning, if not necessarily in terms of play. He would never have regarded himself as being as good a footballer as Giggs, although Ryan always openly admitted that he believed Speed to be the most important player for Wales.

"We each enjoy playing football, which is one of the big keys, really," Speed once explained, as both continued to defy age with match-winning displays. "As soon as that appetite dwindles, it will be time to knock it on the head. I actually started out my career with Leeds as a tricky winger, quick, up and down, although not as good as Ryan. One thing that does happen as time goes on is that you lose that yard of speed, but you can make up for it with speed of thought in your head and by continuing to try to get an edge by embracing these new ideas."

Both men became a football centurion nine times over, but even Giggs, in his later years with Manchester United, never featured in as many matches per season as Speed himself managed at a similar age.

Although Giggs continued to make a huge impact upon Manchester United, as he approached his mid- to late thirties he was picked far more sparingly by Sir Alex Ferguson, either not starting every match or being substituted in some of the ones in which he did. It was only when Speed finally succumbed to a back problem at the grand old age of 39, eventually forced to retire from playing after a year's absence, that he had any real length of time away from the game due to injury. Indeed his only other injury-plagued season came with Newcastle in 2002–03, when was forced to undergo surgery for hernia and groin problems. Even then, he featured in 41 matches for club and country during that campaign, so his absence would have been barely noticeable.

The following season (when in his 35th year, it should be pointed out), Speed made up for any lost time by playing an astonishing 61 games out of a possible 62. That tally was made up of 38 starts in 38 Premier League matches, two out of two Champions League games, two out of two FA Cup appearances, one out of one in the League Cup, seven out of seven Wales internationals and 11 out of 12 possible UEFA Cup games. The only match to be missed was a UEFA Cup tie against NAC Breda in Holland. His Newcastle manager, Sir Bobby Robson, deemed Speed could be rested from that second-leg tie, given that he had already helped Newcastle win the first leg 5-0 at St James' Park and thus their passage into the next round was already secured.

While those were the most number of games Speed played in any one season, it was typical for him to feature in just about every fixture his team was playing over a 20-year career. In the preceding years he had broken the 50-match-per-season barrier three times while with Newcastle, displaying extraordinary and perhaps unprecedented levels of fitness for a footballer at the cutting edge of the British game.

He had first begun those ever-present records as a youngster with Leeds and pretty much kept it going right to the end. In his 36th year, by then as a Bolton player, he played in every Premier League match of the 2004–05 campaign (38 out of 38 again), two out of a possible two FA Cup ties and five out of five Wales internationals. In his 38th year (the 2006–07 season), he was again a Premier League ever-present. Then, in his 39th year (featuring for Bolton in the Premier League and Sheffield United at the top end of the Championship), he still played in 39 matches. Is it any wonder, on examination of these statistics, that Speed set new landmarks to push him close to the iconic Paolo Maldini and which only Giggs has gone on to eclipse in the British game? Was it pure luck, or perhaps down to the way he looked after himself so carefully for all those years away from the field of play?

His own attitude towards the records that he was constantly setting never really changed, though. "Look, it is not something of which I take a lot of notice, but don't mark me down as some sort of old codger!" was always the standard response. He explained that appearing in so many matches over such a long period of time underlined the fact that the lessons he had learned early on from Strachan were clearly the right ones. That pleased him far more than having an individual record to his name.

Shortly after Speed's death, FA Premier League officials announced they would hold a public vote on the greatest player to have graced the League during its first 20 years. A shortlist of 10 players was drawn up. Inevitably both Giggs and Shearer made it into that elite group, as did Cristiano Ronaldo, Eric Cantona, Roy Keane and Paul Scholes (all Manchester United), the Arsenal trio of Dennis Bergkamp, Patrick Vieira and Thierry Henry, plus Gianfranco Zola of Chelsea. Despite his record-breaking feats, Speed did not make it onto the list – nor indeed, knowing him, would he have wanted to have his name placed directly beside such genuine icons of the game. What would have been truly fascinating would have been to have heard his views on who should top the list, for no one would have been better placed to discuss the highs and lows of the Premier League era.

As a player, Speed was very different in his make-up to any of the top 10, but if you were to ask some of the iconic figures who did make the official list to compile one of their own, the name of Gary Speed would almost certainly be considered. If not as the most skilful player, then certainly as one of the most effective and dependable Premier League footballers they ever played with, or against.

Speed's agent Hayden Evans says without hesitation: "Gary leaves behind a lasting legacy. From a football point of view, I believe all coaches of young players should hold up Gary as an example of how people should play the game. He was proof you can have a long and hugely successful career at the highest level without getting involved in the histrionics or attracting the wrong type of headlines.

"I first got to know him when he was a youngster at Leeds just beginning to make the grade. I met Gary's parents, Roger and Carol, got on very well with them and the decision was made that I would represent their son. We quickly developed a friendship, which in my case was easy because there was everything to like about Gary. He was the consummate professional when he needed to be, which is why he lasted the test of time at the highest level, but he could also let his hair down in private and be one of the lads.

"The thing that impressed me about Gary is that despite the niceties, how he could be everything to all men, he was also very single-minded and shrewd. I just got the impression with Gary that while he only wanted to play football, he could have turned his hand to any other walk of life and been just as successful."

3

Destined for the Top

"Even though [Gary] was smaller than the rest... he was put straight into the team and inevitably shone."
Cledwyn Ashford – the schoolmaster who helped discover Gary's football talents

The small town of Queensferry nestles on the Dee Estuary in north-east Wales. It is bordered by Shotton to the west, Sandycroft to the east and Hawarden to the south, which together help make up the area known as Deeside. The English border is just two miles away. Covering an expanse of 10 miles and with a population of around 32,000, Deeside is very much an industrial conurbation, with Corus Construction & Industrial (CCI) steel manufacturers, the Airbus aircraft-making company and the Toyota car plant providing employment for the local population. Other leading companies with bases in the vicinity include the Iceland food chain and the Redrow housebuilding giant.

The town of Wrexham is 12 miles to the south, with Chester just across the border via the A55 dual carriageway, otherwise known locally as the "North Wales Expressway". Liverpool, via the Wirral and the Mersey Tunnel, is approximately 18 miles away to the north. At first glance, this particular part of Wales would not be anyone's idea of a football hotbed. Its most famous inhabitant was perhaps William Gladstone, the four-times British prime minister of the Victorian era, who lived out his latter days until his death at the age of 88 in Hawarden Castle. In more recent times, however, the area has become synonymous with producing a whole glut of modern-day football legends, Gary Andrew Speed among them.

He was brought up in Courtland Drive, in the Aston Park area of Queensferry – in the house where his parents, Roger and Carol Speed, still reside. Gary Speed was just one of a crop of iconic 1980s and 1990s football figures who first kicked a ball around the streets in that area of north Wales. Others hailing from the immediate vicinity include Kevin Ratcliffe, twice captain of the Everton title-winning team of the mid-1980s, who lived just down the road in Ewloe. As a kid, Speed used to do a paper round (Ratcliffe's home among his deliveries) and he would sometimes be chided by the Welsh legend for not getting the paper to him in time to read before morning training.

Michael Owen, who won 89 caps for England, scoring 40 goals, was brought up in Hawarden. Born across the border in the Countess of Chester hospital of an English father, he technically never qualified to play for Wales at senior level, although the whole of his age-group football was through the Welsh system and he would go on to eclipse schools records set by Speed himself. A short drive further up the road is Flint, hometown of Ian Rush, a true Wales and Liverpool legend, who broke all manner of scoring records for club and country. Just a few miles south is Wrexham, hometown of the Manchester United and Wales icon Mark Hughes (or "Sparky" as he was affectionately known from his early north Wales schooldays). Other leading Welsh football figures of the time also hailing from the area included Robbie Savage, Micky Thomas and Joey Jones.

Quite why the area has been such a breeding ground for top-quality sporting talent is open to opinion. Perhaps it's just coincidence; maybe the coaching from school tutors and football officials is extra-special in north-east Wales; or is it merely a natural hunting ground for the big Manchester and Merseyside Premier League clubs – Manchester United, Manchester City, Liverpool and Everton? Most likely it's a mixture of all three, but given Gary Speed's subsequent achievements in the game, he certainly stands next to Rush, Hughes and Owen as one of the region's genuine modern-day greats.

The young Speed was never the biggest or the strongest player, according to former headmaster Cledwyn Ashford, the man who first helped discover his sporting talents. However, at the tender age of eight he embarked on his incredible knack of breaking football records – a characteristic that would remain with him for the next 34 years, as both a Premier League and a Wales player and right through to his last game in charge of his country, when statistically he became Wales's most successful manager.

Born in the local hospital at Mancot, Speed was brought up in a loving family environment, living in Courtland Drive with his parents, Roger and Carol, and sister, Lesley, who was a couple of years older. They were always incredibly supportive to the youngest member of the Speed household and were always to be seen at matches in which he played.

His future wife Louise, also hailed from the area and in due course she and Gary became childhood sweethearts, going on to get married at the local church in 1996 and having their two children together.

Speed's father, Roger, held down a job in the fire service, but he spent most of his free time transporting his talented football-mad son to and from matches, starting at an early age in primary school.

As a pupil of Queensferry Primary School, Speed joined the crack Deeside Schools Representative team at eight years of age, the youngest child ever to do so (the only other player subsequently to match that feat being Michael Owen). The Deeside Schools XI, made up of the best pupils from the primary schools in the area, was ostensibly meant to be a team for 11-year-olds in Year 6, the final year before secondary school. However, Gary's talents were spotted early on by Mr Ashford, chairman of the Flintshire Schools FA, and the late Ron Bishop, founder of Deeside Primary Schools FC and one of the forerunners of quality football anywhere in England and Wales.

Deeside competed against opposition throughout the UK and, despite being three years younger than the other boys, at an age when size and physical growth really did matter, young Gary never once looked out of place or not up to the challenge. Despite being the smallest boy on the pitch, he refused to allow himself to be pushed off the ball, won more than his fair share of headers and made sure his superior ability shone through.

"Ron Bishop could tell at that very early age just how special Gary was," recalls Ashford, headmaster of Bryncoch Primary School in the region for 23 years. "Even though he was smaller than the rest and only in Year 4, he was put straight into the team and inevitably shone. In Year 5, the progression continued and he even captained the side, as he did throughout Year 6 as well – his final year in primary school football. Gary's last match for us, in fact, was in 1981 as captain of the team when we won the Jersey Festival tournament, lifting a trophy called the Tom Yeoman Shield. This is the most prestigious primary school competition in Welsh football and it was a real honour for us to win it."

Altogether Speed made a record 100-plus appearances for the Deeside team, comfortably eclipsing the previous best figure attained. His own games record was then overhauled by Michael Owen, who followed his lead in playing for the team at eight years of age and also went on to break the all-time Deeside Schools scoring record previously set by Ian Rush. Welsh legend "Rushie" showed his early scoring prowess with 72 goals for the team; Owen finished on 79.

Ashford smiles. "I'm convinced Ron Bishop put on more games so Michael could get Gary's appearances record! But look, joking aside, we had a very fine team and a lot of those players who went on to make big names for themselves – Gary Speed, Michael Owen, Ian Rush, Kevin Ratcliffe – first appeared for us. Deeside Primary Schools was at that time one of the best association youth teams in Britain and while Gary played for us in midfield, we could tell he was comfortable in any position. If we needed a goal, we would put Gary up front and invariably he would score that goal for us.

"He was a lot more than just our best player at the time, though. I still recall how, as our under-11s captain, he would stand up at after-match ceremonies to thank parents, sponsors and administrators for their support. It was incredible for one so young. At the Jersey tournament that we won, a man associated with Reading Primary Schools called David Downs came up to me to say he couldn't believe the speech made by our captain and the maturity he had shown. That was Gary for you – even at that age, he did a fantastic job of leading the team, both on and off the pitch. It was so easy to tell Gary was destined for great things, regardless of what he chose to do. He was a very bright lad, always made sure he looked after himself well and had a very wise head on his young shoulders."

At every single match Speed played in, his parents, Roger and Carol, and sister, Lesley, could be spotted on the sidelines, offering their encouragement. "They never missed a game. Gary had huge support from his family, who did all they could to support his progress, whatever the weather conditions, wherever the match," says Ashford.

Speed's development at representative level followed its natural course – to a certain degree, that was – as he moved to Hawarden High School (the comprehensive also attended by Michael Owen) and earned representative honours at Flintshire under-13, under-14 and under-15 levels. He also played, and starred, for the North Wales under-15s team, so the next logical step was to compete for Wales Schoolboys at that level, the highest honour a teenager could have at that stage of his football career.

Wales played England, Scotland and Northern Ireland on a regular basis and Speed was a shoo-in for the team, or so everyone – not least Mr Ashford – presumed. Incredibly, he did not even make it through the trials, although perhaps that says more about the judgement of the selectors rather than being anything to do with his playing ability. By now he had progressed from a local team called Aston Park Rangers FC to a club named Pegasus, also known as Blue Star, who were in effect a satellite side associated with Manchester City, which had been set up to attract and groom the best schoolboys from the area for stardom. Clearly, Speed – who was also interesting Leeds United, as well as Manchester City – was highly regarded, but that still wasn't enough to earn him a Wales Schools cap.

Mr Ashford takes up this somewhat extraordinary tale: "I took him to the Welsh trials, held at the Pilkington ground in St Asaph, and I was obviously very, very confident Gary would be selected for Wales. He was the best player, it naturally followed he would stand out. Unfortunately, the selectors did not pick him and I was very annoyed, to say the least, making my views known to them in no uncertain terms.

"I was told the reason he didn't get in was because of his size. As I've already mentioned, he was not the biggest of boys. Yet despite that, he was still the best header of a ball of the lot, by a mile. He had a great spring in the air which enabled him to get above bigger boys to win his aerial duels, he possessed a great shot, two great feet, could score goals and create them, yet still he was overlooked, because in those days the selectors wanted bigger, stronger boys. These days someone like Gary would just sail through because the selection criteria are different – not then, and he was absolutely gutted.

"I told him that in my view they were biased towards others, explained why, physically, they went for different boys and emphasized my belief that he would go on to become a top footballer, not just a professional player but a quality player at the very highest level. He didn't just have the ability to succeed but the right attitude, too. I hope I managed to lift his spirits a little bit, but I'd be lying if I said he wasn't downhearted at what had just happened, because he understandably was."

In Gary Speed's case, the irony was that he was chosen to represent his country at cricket at Welsh Schools level, yet not in his preferred and more specialist sport. Those who knew him at the time believe he could also have made the grade as a professional cricketer, had he chosen to go down that path, for he was a top bowler and a more than useful batsman. Speed also viewed himself as a pretty decent rugby union player, back then.

"Well, I did until we played a team from south Wales in a representative game," he once told me, smiling at the memory. "We comfortably beat most sides that we played from the north Wales area and thought we were pretty tasty. Then we came up against a side from Glamorgan in a schools semi-final and still fancied our chances. They had youngsters like Neil Jenkins and a few others in their line-up, who went on to play rugby for Wales. We lost 92-0 – and were lucky to get nil! That was the end of any thoughts of me taking rugby seriously. It was football after that for me, with a bit of cricket thrown in during the summer."

Speed may not have been required by Welsh Schools, but Leeds United were soon demanding his services. The fallen Yorkshire giants, a dominant force of British football at the start of the 1970s, were at that time managed by the legendary Billy Bremner and actively courted Speed. His astonishing form for Pegasus, and the various age-group teams for whom he was playing, had caught the eye of the Elland Road scouts, who were keen to reimplement a successful youth policy at Leeds. Fresh out of school, Speed left north Wales for the first time and as a teenager lived in digs in west Yorkshire after signing apprenticeship forms for the club.

It's hard enough for any youngster venturing out into the big wide world, particularly those brought up in the comfortable and homely environment of Wales. It can be even tougher in the cut-throat world of professional football, where dreams are shattered in an instant with a manager telling a young player that he is not good enough to make the grade. Managers up and down the land admit that this is the hardest part of their job. For budding teenage footballers, it can be heartbreaking. Speed was entering the unknown and therefore needed a comforting arm around his shoulder. It came in the shape of Peter Swan, the more seasoned professional for whom he was meant to act as boot boy.

Boot boys are now seen as a relic of the past, but in the old days apprentice footballers had to learn the dressing-room trade the hard way. In between regular training sessions to hone their skill levels, they were instructed to sweep the terraces, tidy the dressing rooms, clean the toilets and wash and polish the muddy boots of a designated first-team player. In return, the apprentice would be given a tip for Christmas to help make up his somewhat measly wage.

Speed is thought to have been one of the last professional footballers to be handed old-style boot boy duties – today's top clubs employ a whole army of backroom staff, including kit men, to perform those sorts of responsibilities – and the player he was instructed to look after was Peter Harold Swan. In fact, Swan was only three years older than Speed and regarded the kid from north Wales as more of a mate than someone designated to keep his boots looking prim and proper for match days. Just a few years earlier, the Leeds-born, tough-talking Yorkshireman signed for the club on schoolboy terms of £25 per week. Capable of playing centre-half or centre-forward, he made an impact on Speed and was one of the early established figures to be looked up to by the budding star.

Swan made his Leeds debut on January 1, 1986 against Oldham and Speed wondered when, or perhaps rather if, he too would get an opportunity to pull on the famous white shirt. "Gary was just a fresh-faced kid with enthusiasm to play football and although he was my boot boy as such, I regarded him more as a friend," recalls Swan. "He was only a couple of years younger than me and I knew it had been a big step for him to leave home and try to settle with us at Leeds. There was inevitable self-doubt in his mind at the time. Gary had seen me break into the Leeds team and he would ask me, 'Do you think I will get my chance?' I replied, 'Of course you will, and once you do get in, you are the sort of kid who will be in the team forever.' It was almost like he needed that reassurance at the time but I could see what a good player he was. This kid was going right to the top, I could tell that straight away.

"For me, it was more about helping him develop as a player and settling him as a person than it was him cleaning my boots spick and span. We trained together every day for two years and I always told Gary it was just a matter of time before he broke into the first team himself."

So, what was the young Speed like at cleaning boots? "Rubbish!" laughs Swan. "Even in those days it was about Gary's self-appearance – how he looked, that sort of thing. He was certainly a good-looking lad throughout his life. I never got in a strop or anything like that, or ever asked him to do the boots again. It was quite tough for some of the youngsters at the club, but I tried to do my bit to ensure Gary was treated with respect, was never the butt of too much mickey-taking or anything like that. I made the time and effort to help him when I could, offer advice, that sort of thing. Look, I could clean my boots myself, couldn't I? Gary was there to learn and he needed someone to hold on to a little, I guess.

"I didn't realize how much of a help I was at the time, but at the end of my career I wrote a book myself and he did a part in it, saying how useful my presence and advice had been for him, To be honest, I was touched by that. I'm just glad I was of assistance. He was a super lad, always prepared to put other people ahead of himself, always willing to listen to and embrace ideas; always destined for the very top. Great player, great person ... and I was right about him being a first-teamer forever once he made his debut, wasn't I?"

Despite the help he was giving Speed, Swan never got to line up in the same first team as his boot boy. Instead he was sold to Hull for £200,000 in March 1989, just a few weeks before his protégé was handed that first-team bow Swan always insisted he would be given. Funnily enough, as with Swan's own debut, Speed's chance to shine also came against Oldham. By that point, Howard Wilkinson (who was to have such a big influence on Speed's career) had taken over the Leeds managerial helm from the unsuccessful Bremner. Wilkinson swiftly sold Swan on to Hull, using the transfer money to buy Gordon Strachan from Manchester United. As the man who had such an early impact on Speed departed, in came another who made an even greater impression. It was Strachan, of course, from whom Speed learned early on what to eat before games and how to prepare to maximize his match-day performance.

Despite being on the cusp of making his Leeds United debut, Speed never forgot those who were there for him at the beginning and first to demonstrate faith in his footballing ability.

"Gary would regularly come back to do presentation evenings for us and we would only have to ask once," says Cledwyn Ashford.

"He would turn up in his Leeds United tracksuit, having won the League Championship, and the kids were overwhelmed to see him give them their own medals. I was in a position to say to them, 'I started where you are at the moment. I wanted to be a professional footballer and have made it. If you have the ability and do the right things, you too may have a chance.'

"The only downside for me is that the late Ron Bishop, who did so much for Gary during his very early days, unfortunately died before he made it with Leeds. Ron would have been so very proud of his achievements. Gary had a wonderful personality and always got on well with everyone. He kept friends with him from his days at Deeside all the way through to his time as Wales manager and wherever he went, whichever club he played for.

"I remained friends with Gary and his family throughout his life and it was always a delight for me to see him. He was an absolutely fantastic ambassador for Deeside. I saw Gary grow from being a little boy into a young man and then a young Wales manager, and he was a very special person with it. He deserved every success he ever had, both as a player and as a manager, and I know everyone in Flintshire was very proud of him and always will be."

In an interview with his local newspaper, shortly after the news of Speed's death, Ashford went on to say: "I am involved with the Wales under-16s and Gary would give his time to come down to the young boys' coaching sessions. The boys appreciated it so much – they would have photos taken with him and he would join in with the fun. He was an inspiration and I referred to him in many changing room talks."

Speed had his first stint at coaching with a local team, the Hawarden Rangers under-eights side, when his son Tommy joined the squad. He helped out for two years and was known simply as "Tommy's dad" rather than Gary Speed, superstar footballer. Hawarden Rangers club secretary Dave Dickel told the *Flintshire Chronicle*: "Gary knew a few of the parents of lads on the team because they were friends of his and he wanted his son to play with them. He was a very approachable bloke and he volunteered to come and help out with the coaching. He was enthusiastic and really got excitement out of doing it.

"You can understand how he took that further with the Welsh squad and inspired them. The children he was coaching were seven or eight and just learning to play. There were good ones and not so good ones, but he treated them all the same. The kids were made up to have him coaching them and it's an experience which will definitely stay with them."

Speed was putting something back into the community which had meant so much to him when he was younger. He had loved his own north Wales football upbringing and the one sour note, which he perhaps never forgot, was the disappointment he felt at not being selected for the Welsh Schools team. Were he still alive, Speed would have noted the irony of his own son Ed being called up for the very same Welsh squad he himself was overlooked for. Today's schools side is under-16s as opposed to under-15s; young Ed earned his selection when he was just 14 years of age.

Ed's selection came less than four months after the death of his father and, of course, fully 28 years after Speed senior had been overlooked at that level. Time has proved that the Welsh selectors clearly made an error, but with some soothing words in his ear from Cledwyn Ashford and others close to him, the young Gary Speed was able to shrug off this setback, refusing to be deterred from his dream. In fact, the adventure was only just beginning for the kid from Queensferry.

4

Leeds United Hero

"We all dream of a team of Gary Speeds..."

Leeds United fans' chant

In exactly the 11th minute of Leeds United's Championship game away to Nottingham Forest, staged at the City Ground two days after Gary Speed's death, the small army of visiting fans who had made the trip down the M1 from Yorkshire broke into a chorus of "Oh, Gary, Gary, Gary, Gary, Gary, Gary, Gary Speed!" They kept on chanting for a full 11 minutes – in recognition of the number on the white shirt worn by Speed when he made his breakthrough as a Leeds player at the end of the 1980s.

Elland Road was where his incredible journey began and what happened that night in Nottingham was quite possibly the most amazing tribute any footballer has been afforded by a set of club supporters anywhere in the world. Ever. As well as chanting that particular song over and over, the Leeds followers also clapped non-stop throughout. As anyone who has ever participated in a one-minute celebration of life will know, towards the end of the 60 seconds, the hands start to sting a little. So just imagine how the Leeds fans at the City Ground must have felt after clapping for a full 11 minutes.

Even Manchester United supporters, Leeds's sworn enemies, posted messages on Facebook, Twitter and internet forums admitting to how bowled over they had been by the special and unique tribute. But that, in a way, summed up Gary Speed: he played for Leeds but was liked, admired and respected by the Old Trafford fans. When he played for Everton, the Liverpool supporters still had time for him. And although he had played for Newcastle, the Sunderland supporters would happily have taken him into the fold as one of their own.

While the 11 minutes of non-stop applause was going on, fans also held up white number 11 shirts bearing a variety of slogans. "Leeds legend, Speed 11," read one. "RIP Speedo," said another. "You're always in our thoughts Gary," stated a third. Towards the end, the chant changed to a more straightforward one of "Speed, Speed, Speed, Speed, Speed!" Then, almost as if it was destiny and the Leeds fans were being rewarded for their fantastic endeavours, midfielder Robert Snodgrass scored. Cue joy among the visiting fans. Leeds went on to win the match 4-0.

Similarly, whenever Spanish club Espanyol play a home tie, their supporters break into applause in the 21st minute as a tribute to one of their former players, Daniel Jarque, who wore the number 21 shirt for the club. Tragically, the 26-year-old midfielder died after suffering a cardiac arrest following a training session in August 2009, but while the tribute from Espanyol fans to Jarque is moving, it doesn't last anywhere near the 11-minute chant afforded to Speed.

Later on at the City Ground, the Leeds fans broke into song once more. This time, to the tune of the Beatles' hit "Yellow Submarine", they chanted:

We all dream of a team of Gary Speeds,
A team of Gary Speeds, a team of Gary Speeds,
We all dream of a team of Gary Speeds,
A team of Gary Speeds, a team of Gary Speeds...

Why were the Leeds followers so emotional that evening? Because Gary Speed was always someone they held close to their hearts. He joined the then fallen Yorkshire giants as a trainee on June 17, 1988 and altogether made 312 appearances for the club, scoring 57 goals over an eight-year period before netting Leeds a cool £3.5 million transfer fee on joining Everton. In anyone's parlance, this represented excellent value for money.

During those history-making years Speed helped Leeds United return to the glory days of old as they won the League Championship in 1992. Silverware had been absent from the Elland Road trophy cabinet since Don Revie's cult heroes last lifted the cup two decades earlier. Speed formed part of a midfield quartet – next to Gordon Strachan, David Batty and Gary McAllister – which is still regarded today as one of the finest in Premier League history. He was a pivotal member of a side that has gone down in Leeds folklore, men who revived the dream and brought the good old days back.

Speed, Strachan, Batty, McAllister and other members of that title-winning team of 1991–92 – the last old First Division Championship before the Premier League era began – may not have achieved quite the legendary status of some of Revie's all-conquering heroes of the 1960s and 1970s. Billy Bremner, Johnny Giles, Allan Clarke, Jack Charlton, Norman Hunter, Peter Lorimer, Terry Cooper, Eddie Gray … Still the names just roll off the tongue. But Gary Speed is bracketed right up there beside those all-time greats in the eyes of the Leeds fans. To this day, they regard him as one of their own. Hence the special 11-minute-long tribute they paid him at the City Ground that night. He became the people's player, which probably means more in the wider scheme of things than any Championship -winning medal.

Gary Cooper, chairman of the Leeds United Supporters Trust, speaks from the heart when he talks about Gary Speed. "What you have to remember about Gary is that while we fully understand he was Welsh, we always viewed him as one of us," says Cooper. "He came through our youth system; he grew up in football terms with us; he was part of the Leeds United family. Ask any Leeds fans and they will tell you that Gary Speed just felt like one of our own.

"We all totally took to Gary from day one. We had been a failing team for some time. All of a sudden we had a dynamo of a midfielder who had come up through our youth ranks and who covered every inch of the pitch in a blink of the eye. What we ask, more than anything else as Leeds fans, is for the players putting on that white shirt to give 100 per cent. We can forgive a lack of quality, provided the effort is there. Gary always gave 110 per cent in every single match without fail.

"He was fearless. It didn't matter if we were playing Manchester United at Old Trafford or Huddersfield Town at Elland Road, he would give everything to the cause and produce the same high level of performance. In football, you often get players who are less talented but make up for that with their commitment; or you get players who are hugely gifted but sometimes aren't as committed as others. You rarely get a player with both qualities, but Gary Speed was one of the exceptions to the rule. He had a great left foot, a terrific shot, was a super passer of the ball and his heading ability was out of this world. When the ball went in the air in either penalty area, we wanted Gary Speed to be on the end of it. We always rated our centre forwards Lee Chapman and Brian Deane as among the finest headers of the ball this club has had. Gary was better than the pair of them and he was a midfielder, not a centre-forward.

"To see a kid coming through at 18 years of age with such flair at the heart of our midfield and beating seasoned professionals with sheer quality was magical. As Speedo broke into the ranks, we turned the corner as a club, following some dark days. It was not the sustained success of the Revie era and no one in that team Gary played in had quite the legendary status of a Bremner or Giles.

"But there are a few others whom we Leeds fans hold extremely close to our hearts. Lucas Radebe, our South African centre-back, was one because of the way he gave everything to the cause. Nigel Martyn was another, a real gentleman who always played with a smile on his face, spoke to the fans and got on well with us. Let me tell you that Gary Speed is another member of that very elite group.

"Just look back at the goals Gary scored for us and you will see another reason why we hold him so dearly in our hearts. Whenever Gary celebrated, you would notice his arms raised towards the fans, not towards his teammates. Of course he wanted to celebrate with them, but his first port of call was the supporters. It was always the other players running towards him because he was facing us, rather than him running towards them. That's why we sang his name non-stop at Nottingham Forest. We wanted his family and friends to know exactly what he meant to us. The Forest match was an absolute tribute to Gary Speed's memory."

It was back on May 6, 1989 when Speed was handed his League debut in the old Second Division by Howard Wilkinson. Indeed the man who would go on to become England caretaker manager for brief periods in 1999 and also 2000 had only joined Leeds a few months before from Sheffield Wednesday, where he had done an excellent job in charge. Wilkinson's switch of Yorkshire clubs came as something of a surprise given that under him Wednesday were stabilized in the top half of the top flight whereas Leeds were near the bottom of the old Second Division, today known as the Championship.

For the Leeds Board of Directors, this was something of a coup, though. A succession of managers had tried – and failed – to restore the heady days of yesteryear under Revie, when those Leeds legends won two League titles, the FA Cup, the League Cup and twice triumphed in the old European Fairs Cup. Brian Clough, Jimmy Armfield, Jock Stein, Jimmy Adamson and three greats from that Revie side – Allan Clarke, Eddie Gray and former skipper supreme Billy Bremner – had each filled the Leeds manager's hot-seat. But the club was very much on the slide, relegated in 1982, and Wilkinson was charged with restoring their fortunes.

He stayed at the helm from 1988 to 1996 and the one playing constant during that time as Leeds returned to winning ways was a young Speed. The debut game on May 6, 1989, when Speed was just 19, was an end-of-season affair against Oldham, played out in front of just 14,459 fans, who witnessed a dreary 0-0 stalemate. The *Yorkshire Post* described the occasion as a pretty nondescript, end-of-season Roses battle, notable for one reason alone: the emergence of Gary Speed. The fresh-faced youngster was selected after scoring in 12 successive Leeds junior matches as well as scoring two goals in a Central League 3-3 draw against Manchester United reserves, just four days earlier. Speed forced a good save from Oldham goalkeeper Andy Rhodes with a low shot. Wilkinson recalls: "Gary acquitted himself very well that day and after just one match was in the team to stay. I saw quite a bit of him playing for the youth team and could tell straight away that he had talent and would go on to carve out a great career for himself."

There was a special rapport between Wilkinson and Speed, mentor and pupil, which would last for many years and this was only the beginning. Wilkinson was the footballing father figure who guided Speed, telling him what to do and, more importantly, what *not* to do. Speed was the new young kid on the block, who brought zest, athleticism and wonderful ability to aid his manager's dream of winning trophies for Leeds United. They were good for each other.

The following season, 1989–90, Leeds won the Second Division title and thus promotion to the top flight. Speed, back then regarded as a marauding left-winger, before settling down as a calmer central midfielder for the remainder of his career, played a key role in that success. He had just turned 20, but played 25 League games that year and scored three pivotal goals, all at the business end of the season when promotions are traditionally won or lost.

For most of the season, it was nip and tuck between Leeds and Yorkshire rivals Sheffield United for top spot in the table and it was Speed's influence that helped Wilkinson's men to seize the initiative in the closing month of the season. He scored crucial goals to help secure precious points in drawn games against Bradford City and Brighton, but the match no one at Elland Road ever forgets was the top-of-the-table showdown with rivals Sheffield United on April 16, 1990.

That Easter Monday, a crowd of 32,727 crammed into the ground for a battle that would make or break Leeds's season. They went into the encounter on the back of a poor run of form, having picked up just two points from their previous four League fixtures. A 10-point lead they once held at the top had now been whittled away to three and Sheffield United arrived in Leeds determined to cut the gap still further.

Cue the Gary Speed show. He calmed Leeds's nerves in setting up the opening goal for Gordon Strachan before racing away with pace and verve down the left to cross for Lee Chapman, who made it 2-0. After Strachan added a third from the penalty spot, Speed then rounded off his team's resounding win with a sublime individual goal. Picking the ball up on the halfway line, he sprinted the remaining length of the pitch before coolly slotting home in the corner of the Sheffield United net to complete a 4-0 triumph.

As Speed bore down on goal that afternoon, the TV commentator John Boyd bellowed out: "Go on, Gary Speed, get one for yourself, son!" His words would later be placed on a flag in Speed's memory at Elland Road.

Speed's stunning showing enabled Leeds to win the League that year. The team secured the title by defeating a Bournemouth team (then managed by a certain Harry Redknapp) 1-0, down on the South Coast. They were back in the big time and any fears they would once more be instantly relegated were banished as Leeds ended the following season in a highly creditable fourth place.

Arsenal and Liverpool filled the top two spots but Leeds had acquitted themselves superbly in the top flight, with Speed proving he deserved to be on that sort of stage, playing 38 matches and scoring seven goals in total. One of those goals came during an opening day of the season 3-2 victory at Everton on August 20, 1991 – surely a bittersweet moment for Speed. Everton were the club he grew up supporting as a boy and there he was, suddenly scoring against them. His efforts helped Leeds to settle into their new environment and, having more than just consolidated, they were ready for another crack at the following season's First Division Championship.

This was the season, 1991–92, when Wilkinson's influence upon Speed was perhaps at its greatest and Speed's impact on proceedings, to help secure the title for Wilkinson and Leeds, was at its zenith. Even though he started the campaign as a 21-year-old, Speed played like an experienced old hand, figuring in 41 out of the 42 League matches Leeds played to land the title and finishing with seven crucial goals to his name. Lee Chapman, with 16, was top scorer. Only goalkeeper John Lukic and midfield maestro Gary McAllister – ever-present during that campaign – made more appearances, but they were significantly older than Speed. For one so young, this was an extraordinary exhibition of stamina, ability and versatility, not to mention maturity. That season, Speed played in every single outfield position at some point.

Wilkinson recalls the manner in which Speed changed positions with a minimum of fuss, always doing so for the sake of the team: "I started him on the left of midfield, moved him to the right when necessary, back to defence, left-back, right-back, centre-back, centre midfield … He even had a go up front. Never once, not even once, did Gary moan or question what I was asking him to do. Sometimes these days when I see top players asked to move out of position during games I notice a shaking of the head, hands on hip, something of a stare. These modern-day footballers could have learned a lot from Gary.

"Why did I ask him to change roles so often? I did it because at the time I thought it best for the team and best for the result. Most importantly, I knew Gary would always give it his best shot. I didn't give him those values and qualities I should point out – I and other managers benefited from them. It was his mum and dad, Roger and Carol, who developed, nurtured and preserved those precious values in Gary through the years. He had integrity, commitment, generosity; he also had a lack of the wrong sort of pride. He took pride in his performance all right, but was never too proud to do less glamorous jobs for the team that I told him needed to be done. That is why, with no fuss whatsoever, he changed positions so often for me and in every single case played to the very highest standard. That underlined just what a very special footballer Gary Speed was.

"He was a player's player, which in a football dressing room is the ultimate mark of respect. The team came first, not 'I', not 'me', not 'Gary'. He was clearly genuine, didn't have tantrums or sulks, he just got on with the game. He turned up every day to throw everything into training, was never late. People used to ask me how many rules I had at a football club and I used to reply, 'As few as possible.' But the most important one of the lot is to make sure you are not late. Gary respected that, never was.

"That year when we won the League he was absolutely magnificent. I remember Bobby Robson taking him to Newcastle several seasons later and asking me what I thought Gary's qualities were. I told him he was signing someone who played football where it mattered. 'What do you mean?' he asked. I replied, 'Gary will play in their penalty box and also in your penalty box; he will defend your goal and he will be effective in front of theirs.' Those two penalty boxes are where it really matters in football, where games are won and lost. Gary would do it where it really counted. He would win headers or block tackles in his own area; he would pop up with a header or score or create a goal in attack. And for good measure, he would also work up and down in between the penalty boxes during the rest of the game, too."

Leeds's title-winning team that year consisted of John Lukic in goal, a back four of Mel Sterland, Chris Fairclough, Chris Whyte and Tony Dorigo, with Lee Chapman and Rod Wallace up front. But it was the midfield quartet of Gordon Strachan, David Batty, Gary McAllister and Speed himself who were seen as the real architects behind the triumph. That midfield possessed everything: the sheer tenacity, doggedness and tackling bite of Batty, Strachan's ability to lead as captain and pull the strings, the sublime passing qualities of McAllister and the energetic youth, pace, endeavour, athleticism and creativity that Speed provided from the left. When he wasn't asked to fill in elsewhere for the team, that is! The balance of that midfield was almost perfection and opposing teams were simply steamrollered aside.

There were a lot of big characters around Speed, but despite his tender years he was never overawed by them and indeed, as an absolute minimum, was an equal partner to his more-famous midfield colleagues. I say minimum, because as Wilkinson points out: "In terms of performing to a consistently high level week in, week out, Gary was the best. A tremendous achievement considering he was also the youngest. At that time he already had everything a manager would want in a player. Alongside his personal qualities, which I've already detailed, he had technical attributes – a great left foot, good passer, tackler, great work-rate, eye for goal – which made him a permanent fixture in my starting XI. He scored goals, and crucial ones, too. He never stopped working, was in the game for the entire 90 minutes. That midfield would be comparable to any of the best around today and would probably get in en bloc into the top sides. Gary was part of something special."

The historic season, which saw Leeds vie with Sir Alex Ferguson's Manchester United aces for the League title, kicked off with a 1-0 victory at Nottingham Forest. There was perhaps something of an omen there, given the manner in which the Leeds fans sang Speed's name so warmly for a full 11 minutes, 20 years on. Leeds remained unbeaten for their first 10 matches, lost the 11th 1-0 at Crystal Palace, but went top for the first time on October 26, with a 1-0 home win over Oldham, the team against which Speed had made his debut, just two years earlier. Over the remainder of the season they were nip and tuck with Manchester United, swapping first and second spots in the run-up to a televised double-header on Sunday, April 26, 1992.

Leeds, who were one point clear at the top of the League, with 76 to Manchester United's 75, played first, away to old foes Sheffield United at Bramall Lane in a noon kick-off, before Sir Alex Ferguson's team went on to tangle with their great rivals Liverpool at Anfield three hours later. The pressure really was on Leeds going into the earlier of the two games. If they lost to their Yorkshire rivals, the title would be out of their reach. A win, on the other hand, and all the pressure would be on Manchester United.

A couple of years earlier, in the win-or-bust shoot-out with Sheffield United for the Second Division title, Speed had come to the fore and helped Leeds win the day by setting up two goals and scoring one himself in a 4-0 victory. This time, on an even bigger stage, he would once more exert a strong influence on proceedings, though in a somewhat fortuitous manner. After Alan Cork had fired Sheffield ahead, a clearance from their centre-back and captain Brian Gayle rebounded off Speed as he looked to close down the ball. It fell into the path of Rod Wallace, who made the score 1-1.

Jon Newsome, who as a fellow youngster was Speed's great friend at the club, was playing right-back that day in place of an injured Mel Sterland and marked the occasion with a goal to put Leeds 2-1 in front. Lee Chapman scored an unfortunate own goal to make it 2-2, but Gayle then put through his own net at the other end to complete a topsy-turvy 90 minutes.

Leeds won 3-2 and were now four points clear of Manchester United. With just one weekend of fixtures left after this, it meant the title would be returning to Elland Road if Liverpool could beat Fergie's men. All eyes now turned to Anfield and Speed travelled to the home of Newsome's parents for some late lunch and to watch on TV with his friend how their rivals for the title fared.

Ian Rush, a Wales teammate of Speed's, scored early and Mark Walters made it 2-0 to Liverpool. The final whistle blew and Leeds were unreachable at the top. As Speed and Newsome celebrated, the mother of all Yorkshire parties began. Still only 22 years of age, Speed was already a League champion and he declared: "This is the happiest I could be in football. To win the League title over the course of a whole season proves you are the best team. It's a brilliant moment.

We just kept going as Manchester United fell away. Our team spirit
– which was fantastic – got us through in the end, I feel."

All's well that ended well, but despite the pure joy that winning the
League title had provided, Wilkinson reveals that during the course
of that season he called Speed into his office for what he dubs "the
longest one-to-one chat I have ever had with any player". During
the mentor-pupil conversation, he emphasized the need for Speed to
make sure he did all the right things away from the pitch and asserted
thta, at the tender age of 22, he should begin to think about one day
becoming a captain and even a manager.

Wilkinson takes up the story: "I sat him down and told him a
number of things that day, pointing out he was an idol in a big city,
was young, very good-looking. 'All those things will attract other
people to you, become positives in your life, and you can use them to
your advantage,' I told him. 'Or all those things can become negatives
in your life and you can abuse them.'

"I went on to say, 'Your career will last only as long as your fitness
– look after your body and it will look after you. Train right, live right
and you'll go on playing, like Gordon Strachan, until you are 40. At the
moment the only thing you think about is coming in here, kicking a ball,
going home and enjoying life, but even though you're still very young,
you've played enough games to start thinking about how to invest in
your career. A lot of players choose not to – the choice is yours.'

"It was a sobering talk for Gary. Life was just a ball at the time
but these were serious points I was making. I pointed out that he
was a natural leader, possessed the qualities to be a captain, then a
coach and then a manager one day. He was not an extrovert but he
was rarely injured, always gave 100 per cent, performed to a high
standard whether the team won, lost or drew, wherever we were
playing, whoever the opposition, whatever the occasion.

"I told him, 'People inside and outside of the game look at you and wish they were like you. That makes you a role model and role models are potential leaders. That makes you a captain at an appropriate time, a coach at an appropriate time and a manager at an appropriate time. But the investment starts right here and now: as you leave this office, you need to make a decision.' At first Gary thought I was joking. Then, when he realized I meant every word, he gave me a sort of embarrassed laugh, which indicated to me he wasn't so sure. I didn't know whether I had convinced him or confused him but fortunately all of those milestones were to become reality. Since that day he grew even further in stature and acquired a personal confidence which marked him out above most others.

"To some people, that step into leadership happens easily. They decide at the end of their career they want to be a manager and are fortunate enough to get a job. But mostly it happens because people have a passion for something. Gary did have that passion and I just wanted him to start using it positively, early on, and begin building for the future."

Wilkinson was also a strong influence when it came to the sports science approach to football, something regarded as revolutionary back in the early 1990s, but which Speed welcomed from day one. He was the first British footballer to truly embrace the high-tech approach in his preparation for matches and on becoming manager of Wales many years later, he brought the modern methods with him into the international game.

"I tried to steer him that way early on," explains Wilkinson. "We were big into analysis and into things such as diet, rehydration, trying to get Gary to perform to the peak of his performance on match days. These days there is lots of back-up for this sort of thing – computer data, printouts and so on – but ours back then was all done manually.

We even spoke to specialists at the local hospital, including the head of the kidney department. If anyone knew about rehydration, it would be them – they were the *real* experts, so we tapped into their knowledge. This sort of sports science approach is accepted as the norm these days but back then, when Gary grew up in the game, it was certainly not commonplace. We had support personnel in the background to give the help we believed top athletes needed.

"Gary was always a practiser; prided himself on learning and getting better. It's an approach modern players are more likely to take on board today but Gary was one of the very first to embrace it back then. I think what he learned with us also helped him when he accepted the Welsh manager's job, which I thought was a big gamble at the time. He knew from his early days with Leeds that 95 per cent of football is about preparation and that was even more relevant at international level where you aren't with the players day in, day out, as you are at a club side.

"When international players do come together what you have to do is be spot-on in getting them prepared properly for the game in the short space of time they are with you. He did that perfectly – he made Wales a 'Gary Speed' team. Part of that would have been drawing on the experience of the different approach we had back in those Leeds days."

Leeds's title triumph was the last of the pre-Premier League boom era. Thus Speed and his Elland Road teammates could proudly say they were the final winners of the old First Division Championship, their final points tally of 82 leaving them four better off than Manchester United.

Alex Ferguson and his men had been desperate to pip Leeds to top spot because this was a trophy that Manchester United had not won since George Best, Bobby Charlton and George Best strutted their stuff under Matt Busby, back in 1967. Since then, Britain's biggest football club had seen Leeds (three times), Manchester City, Everton (three times), Arsenal (three times), Derby (twice), Liverpool (11 times), Aston Villa and Nottingham Forest crowned England's finest while they themselves kicked their heels in frustration. Now, following their defeat by Leeds and stung at this failure, Ferguson made it his mission to right the wrong. And so he put together a gifted crew of individuals who ensured Manchester United won no fewer than seven of the first nine Premier League titles, with only Kenny Dalglish's Blackburn Rovers and Arsène Wenger's Arsenal momentarily halting the relentless red bandwagon.

Ironically, Ferguson's cause was helped by Wilkinson's controversial decision to sell him Leeds's newish striker Eric Cantona for £1.2 million towards the end of November 1992, a move that caused outcry among the Elland Road fans. Cantona, who had joined Leeds for £900,000 from French football, played a handful of matches in the Championship-winning year and with Leeds now in the European Cup, his extra quality was expected to really come to the fore and further bolster the already talented squad as the 1992–93 season commenced.

What a start he made too, smashing home a magnificent hat-trick in his very first game as Leeds beat Liverpool 4-3 four months after their title triumph to lift the Charity Shield in what was Speed's first appearance at Wembley. In doing so, Cantona joined an elite group of players to score a Wembley hat-trick and for a while briefly matched Speed for popularity among the Leeds fans, who came up with the famous "Ooh, ah, Cantona! Say ooh, ah, Cantona!" chant in his honour. However, Leeds began to dip downwards whereas Manchester United headed off in the opposite direction. Cantona was a match-winning wizard for them once he completed his move across the Pennines, while a young Welshman called Ryan Giggs broke through to pep up the side with his flair, energy and ability from the left wing in much the same way as Speed had done with Leeds the previous year.

Wilkinson's team were unable to even come close to defending their Championship crown and finished in a disappointing 17th place. Lee Chapman was the only player to reach double figures in goals, scoring 13 in the League. Despite the general malaise, Speed continued his development as a footballer and netted seven goals from the 39 matches in which he featured during that season. He also produced what Leeds fans view as another of his finest performances in the white number 11 shirt in a European Cup tie against German champions VfB Stuttgart on September 30, 1992. Leeds lost the first leg 3-0 in Germany and mission improbable was how it must have seemed for the return clash, two weeks later.

The Leeds players responded by rampaging to a 4-1 victory at Elland Road, with Speed very much to the fore as he scored the opening goal after 11 minutes. Thereafter, he had a huge role to play as further efforts from Gary McAllister, Eric Cantona and Lee Chapman at least ensured the score was level 4-4 on aggregate. Leeds were out on the away-goal rule or so they thought but at least some pride had been restored. Amazingly, it was then revealed that Stuttgart had fielded an ineligible player. In those days, UEFA insisted on a three-foreigners-only rule for teams competing in European competitions. Stuttgart coach Christoph Daum infringed that regulation when, with eight minutes to go and three non-Germans already in his line-up, he sent on Serbian Jovica Simanić as a substitute.

Clearly UEFA had to act and they awarded the game 3-0 to Leeds, which made it 3-3 on aggregate and meant a replay had to take place on neutral territory. Leeds won 2-1 at Barcelona's Nou Camp nine days afterwards and progressed to round two, only to lose home and away to Glasgow Rangers later that October in a tie dubbed the Battle of Britain and won 4-2 on aggregate by the Scots.

The following season Speed had his best year for scoring goals, hitting 10 as Leeds got back on track to finish fifth in the League, a feat they repeated the next season as well. By this stage, though, the team he had grown up with was beginning to change. Lee Chapman, now well into his mid-thirties, had had the best days of his career and was replaced by Brian Deane, Speed's friend Jon Newsome was sold to Norwich for £1 million and, perhaps more surprisingly, David Batty was permitted to join Blackburn for a record £2.75 million fee. At the end of the 1995–96 campaign that figure would be eclipsed when Speed himself was transferred to Everton, the club he had always supported as a boy, in a £3.5 million deal. Wilkinson would soon follow him out of the Elland Road door.

Leeds finished the season in 13th position and while they reached Wembley again, this time in the League Cup Final on March 24, 1996, it was a disappointing anticlimax as they crashed to a 3-0 defeat against Aston Villa. In fact, they won just two of their last 16 matches, lost six in a row at one stage and, according to one Leeds director at the time, Wilkinson was under pressure to sell players.

"The bank was putting pressure on the club to raise revenue to pay off debts. Gary Speed was one of the players Leeds could sell to find that sort of money," recalls Peter Ridsdale, who went on to become club chairman a few years later. "There is no way Howard wanted to sell Gary. He was very close to his players and particularly to Gary, who was with him pretty much from start to finish. But there was a bit of a boardroom power struggle going on at the time and Howard's hands were tied. Everton wanted Gary and a deal was done to sell him to them. Gary never wanted to leave but he had to because of the mess off the field."

Thus, on April 29, 1996, a Tuesday, Gary Speed appeared in Leeds United colours for the last time. It wasn't a great ending, with Leeds losing 1-0 at home to Newcastle, but no one will ever forget the impact he had on the club during his eight years at Elland Road. He departed having scored 39 goals in 248 League matches, 11 further goals in 26 League Cup ties, five in 21 FA Cup games and two in European and other matches. His return of 57 goals from 312 games was splendid for a midfield player, but he brought infinitely more to Leeds United FC than mere records.

Wilkinson explains: "Leeds is a one-club city and there aren't too many like that of such a large size in the UK. You've got Newcastle, I guess, where Gary also played, but generally it's hard to find cities of that sort of population and commercial opportunity, where you only have one football club. Thus, when the football team starts to show anything of note, as we did, the players become part of the folklore and fabric of the whole city. During Gary's time at Leeds we enjoyed an incredible rise which, if I'm being honest, I would have preferred to have been more gradual. He was the youngest member of that team to play so regularly for us and the fans had a natural affinity with him."

"Gary was one of our own and with him we won the Championship, the old Division Two title, played at Wembley and enjoyed success again," says Gary Cooper, chairman of the Leeds Supporters Trust. "He encapsulated everything Leeds United fans wanted in a player – he was the first, second and third to the ball. He was a real hero to us. It is why we all used to sing, 'We all dream of a team of Gary Speeds'. It didn't matter where Gary went afterwards – Everton, Newcastle, Bolton or Sheffield United – he never, ever stopped being part of us."

Upon learning of Speed's death, a Leeds United fans forum organized a collection and with the funds purchased a giant Leeds flag, which bears the slogan "Go on, Gary Speed, get one for yourself, son". The words were exactly the same as those used by the commentator John Boyd when Speed scored that solo wonder-goal in the old Second Division title decider against Sheffield United.

The flag was duly marched around the ground on December 3, 2012, when Millwall visited Leeds – the first game to be played at Elland Road after Speed's death. That afternoon, his widow, Louise, sons, Ed and Thomas, and parents, Roger and Carol, made the moving pilgrimage to where it had all begun, 24 years earlier. They were shown an enormous number of wreaths and bouquets left in tribute by the Billy Bremner statue just outside the ground. The flag itself has been donated to the museum in Elland Road's East Stand and is there for visitors to see, while a hospitality suite was renamed with immediate effect and is known today as the Gary Speed Suite.

The Leeds legend may have gone but he will never be forgotten by those at Elland Road who continue to dream of "a team of Gary Speeds".

5

A Boyhood Dream Fulfilled

"The only time I'm not an Evertonian is in the 90 minutes I play against them."

Gary Speed

Nil satis nisi optimum (Nothing but the best is good enough) is the motto for Everton Football Club. For Gary Speed, those words could hardly have been more appropriate as he bade farewell to Leeds United in the summer of 1996 and put pen to paper on a five-year deal at Goodison Park. For him, it was a dream come true, because Everton were the club he grew up supporting as a boy. To Speed, they were simply the best, nothing less. During kickabouts with his mates on the streets and in the parks of Deeside as a youngster, he always imagined himself to be playing in the famous blue shirt with the Everton badge and accompanying Latin motto that adorned it. Suddenly that dream was to become true and he would pull on the shirt for real.

In north Wales, there is enormous support for Everton (and Liverpool and Manchester United, for that matter), with thousands of fans making the short hop across the border to watch one of the big three on Saturday afternoons. Speed struck upon Everton as the club he wanted to follow. Among his earliest idols were Kevin Ratcliffe and Neville Southall ("Big Nev"), two Goodison Park and Wales legends that he would later line up beside in his country's red. The two had been at the centre of Everton's golden era of the mid-1980s, when the Blues were arguably the best team in Europe, only denied the opportunity to conclusively prove that fact in the European Cup owing to the ban imposed on English clubs at the time following the Heysel tragedy of 1985. The loss of life of so many Juventus fans at the European Cup Final against Liverpool led to UEFA banning English clubs, which meant that in their hey-day, Everton could not compete in the most prestigious club competition of the lot.

Under Howard Kendall, Ratcliffe captained the Everton side that won two League titles (1985 and 1987), an FA Cup at Wembley (1984) and also the European Cup Winners' Cup, which they lifted in 1985 as a result of defeating the Austrians of Rapid Vienna 3-1 in the final in Rotterdam. At the time, Big Nev was commonly viewed as the greatest goalkeeper in the world, his incredible shot-stopping exploits breaking the hearts of opposing strikers and thus ensuring that game after game was won by the Toffees.

For Speed, the Everton team rolled off the tongue: Neville Southall, Gary Stevens, Derek Mountfield, Kevin Ratcliffe, Pat van den Hauwe, Trevor Steven, Peter Reid, Paul Bracewell, Kevin Sheedy, Graeme Sharp, Andy Gray ... Later, others such as Gary Lineker, Dave Watson, Alan Harper and Ian Snodin would be added to the mix. For a football-mad teenager, those were halcyon days to be cheering on the Everton side. However, as Speed grew older and he himself began conquering British football with title-winning Leeds at the beginning of the 1990s, so Everton started to fall on harder times. They did win the FA Cup once more, for the fifth time in their history, by defeating Manchester United 1-0 in the 1995 final, but their manager of the time, Joe Royle, wanted much more. Signing Gary Speed, now in his mid-twenties and approaching his peak as a player, in a £3.5 million deal was meant to be part of that equation, a big part.

Speed didn't take long in agreeing to make the full-time switch back across the Pennines, knowing it meant that he could live close to his north Wales roots (from his hometown of Queensferry, it is only a short drive up to Liverpool via the Wirrall, and through the Mersey Tunnel). But it wasn't about coming home: it was living the fantasy for real and giving his football fresh momentum after it had gone somewhat stale at Elland Road. "Everton was always my club – I used to come across from north Wales to watch them play from around the age of 12. My dream was to play for the club and it's never really faded," he announced happily. "Maybe I stayed at Leeds one or two seasons too long. Maybe I need a move to get my career going again, but that's all behind me. I look forward with optimism towards the future now."

Everton proved to be a fresh beginning, and in more ways than one. As well as joining a new team, Speed also switched positions to become a permanent central midfield player at the hub of the action. With Leeds, he first made his name as a rampaging wide player down the left – one with the zip, athleticism and energy to charge along the flank and whip over goal-creating crosses for others to convert. Though he never possessed incredible pace, for a while he was sharp and canny enough to get away from opposition full-backs. As Speed grew older, he settled on a role that relied on his football brain rather than any out-and-out speed he may have possessed. "I never did have much pace to lose!" he laughed. But he still retained the energy to race up and down the pitch – as Howard Wilkinson once said, "Doing it in the two penalty boxes where it really mattered" – in the centre of midfield, however, he now became more of the team orchestrator.

Royle built the side around his new capture from Leeds. He knew Speed could pass the ball short, he could pass it long, was equally comfortable passing it off his right or left foot and had the bravado to mix it with opposition midfield hard men, should they wish to turn the game from the beautiful variety to a more combative encounter. Throw into the cocktail his imperious heading ability, his knack of popping up with key goals, plus his work-rate and endeavour, and he was pretty much the prototype of what a modern midfielder needed to be.

With Leeds, Speed had already proved that he had an uncanny knack of shining on the big occasion, so it was perhaps inevitable he should mark his Everton debut with a goal, helping his team to a 2-0 win over Newcastle United at Goodison Park on August 17, 1996. The build-up to the match was dominated by the Newcastle debut of Toon idol Alan Shearer. At the time, the Geordie men were flying under Kevin Keegan, another Tyneside hero, and the signing of Shearer, next to David Ginola and Les Ferdinand, was meant to be the one to deliver the Premier League title.

Just a couple of months earlier, Shearer had been top scorer at the Euro '96 Championships staged in England as the Three Lions team, managed by Terry Venables, marched on to the semi-finals, only to agonizingly lose to Germany in another of those dreaded penalty shoot-outs. With goals against the Germans, Holland (two), Scotland and Switzerland during the tournament, Shearer had done enough to become football's hottest property. A few weeks on, when Kevin Keegan signed him from Blackburn Rovers, the £15 million fee paid almost doubled the previous highest British transfer record: Liverpool's £8.5 million to land Stan Collymore from Nottingham Forest.

The signing of Shearer, top scorer at the recent Euro '96 Championships, for Newcastle United, was big, *big* news. A proud Geordie, he was going home to play for the team that he himself had once supported as a boy from the terraces, just as Gary Speed was about to appear in his first match for the side he had followed as a youngster. Now the stage was set for Shearer to mark his Newcastle bow with a goal that would send the travelling "Toon Army" crazy with excitement, but instead he was quietened by Everton's centre-backs, Dave Watson and David Unsworth, and it was Speed who stole the show, dancing through the Newcastle defence after 40 minutes to score his own debut goal and supplement an earlier penalty, which Unsworth converted in front of a sell-out crowd.

It took an awful lot to upstage Shearer in those days and although Speed had managed that commendable feat, somewhat typically he regarded the three points secured for Everton with his goal as being far more important. Already he had made his mark with the Everton fans and two draws in the next couple of matches (against Manchester United and Tottenham) were further decent results. So, could Everton build on this fine start? The answer was no, as Speed quickly came to discover. He realized that the team he had joined lacked the necessary balance and creativity, and there wasn't much of a cutting edge up front either. Everton's results would quickly fade away as they lost successive matches to Aston Villa, Wimbledon and Middlesbrough. However, the players got the results back on track with wins over Sheffield Wednesday, West Ham, Nottingham Forest and Leicester. Speed was to have two of his finest moments in an Everton shirt in the space of four November days. On Saturday, November 16, 1996 he smashed home the first – and what would prove the only hat-trick – of his career as Royle's team thumped Southampton 7-1 in front of 35,669 ecstatic Goodison Park fans.

"Southampton demolished by Speed of Light," declared the following day's headlines. The Southampton side, managed by Graeme Souness, didn't know what had hit them. Speed set up Graham Stuart for Everton's opening goal and after Andrei Kanchelskis added a second, the Welsh ace hammered home a quick-fire double himself.

Kanchelskis grabbed a second of his own, while Nick Barmby made it six before Speed rounded off the scoring with the third of what the press dubbed "a brilliant hat-trick".

"This is the best performance since I came here," beamed Royle afterwards. "Everyone played well, but Gary Speed was Man of the Match for his goals – a great effort from a top player!"

Four days on, Speed was once more on target, this time at Anfield in the Merseyside derby against Liverpool as he grabbed a late equalizer to earn Everton a 1-1 draw. What's more, the goal came in front of the Kop. For a diehard Everton fan, which Speed was of course, as well as being their star player, this was the stuff of fairy tales. For an Evertonian, it doesn't get much better than celebrating a decisive goal at the Kop end of the home of your long-standing rivals.

Things were understandably buoyant that Wednesday evening as the Everton team coach left Anfield, but the somewhat golden four-day period was as good as it would get during a 1996–97 campaign which petered out in disappointing fashion, with Everton tailing away to finish a lowly 16th in the Premier League table. In fact, "petered out" is putting it mildly: Everton went into freefall, at one stage losing six matches in a row to find themselves dragged deep into the relegation mire.

At the end of March, Royle left the manager's post by mutual consent and veteran centre-half Dave Watson was installed as interim boss until the end of the season, tasked with securing the results which would enable the double League title winners of just a decade earlier to avoid the ignominy of being relegated out of the top flight for the first time since the 1950s. For Speed the prospect of his beloved Everton going down was unthinkable; the dreaded drop was only avoided by the skin of their teeth.

Everton managed just one win in their last 12 matches – at home to Tottenham on April 12, 1997 – but it was a priceless victory. The three points accrued that afternoon enabled the Toffees to finish on 42 points, two clear of Sunderland, who were relegated with 40 points. Were it not for the 1-0 triumph over Spurs, the unthinkable might have become a horror reality. Guess who scored the winning goal that day at Goodison? That's right: Gary Speed, with a brilliant diving header. Cometh the hour, cometh the man, as they say.

In contrast to Everton's fortunes, the Newcastle team Speed's goal had helped to defeat nine months earlier on the opening day of the season had recovered sufficiently to finish second in the Premier League, denied the title by Manchester United. Shearer predictably scored a glut of goals in his debut season, but so too did Speed in his first campaign with the new club, finishing joint top scorer with centre-forward Duncan Ferguson on 11 goals. For a midfielder to manage that many in a struggling team – one goal every four games – was an excellent achievement. Speed, who appeared in 41 matches, was unanimously named Everton's Player of the Year. Even in his most optimistic moments when kicking a ball about as a kid growing up in north Wales, he could never really have imagined that honour would be bestowed on him.

Happy though he was with the prestigious individual gong, Speed was more concerned about the fact that he had just been involved in what would turn out to be the only relegation battle of his playing career and he didn't want a repeat of those concerns as the 1997–98 campaign approached. Meanwhile, for Everton the first issue to be resolved was Royle's full-time successor. Perhaps somewhat surprisingly, the man to whom the Everton board now turned was the tried-and-trusted Howard Kendall, who had been at the helm during those title-winning years in the mid-1980s. At the beginning of the 1990s, he had also had a second, far less successful spell in charge, with his best days at the club perceived by many to be behind him.

Having marvelled from the terraces at the manner in which Kendall's first Everton team rose to the top, Speed, at least, would have been excited at the prospect of working under the man who himself had been a silky midfielder for the club a few decades earlier, starring next to England World Cup winner Alan Ball. Even more so when, with just an hour to go before the start of the season, a home game against Crystal Palace, out of the blue Kendall told Speed he was relieving Dave Watson of the Everton captaincy and instead giving the job to him.

It was a huge call. Local lad Watson was something of an Everton legend, eventually making 419 appearances for the club and always wearing his heart on his sleeve whenever he pulled on that blue shirt. As a no-nonsense centre-back who gave 100 per cent commitment in every match and was vociferous in barking out orders to his teammates, he was clearly captaincy material. However, Kendall instantly spotted leadership qualities in Speed as well and became the first manager to give him the responsibility of wearing the armband, a move subsequently followed by a number of others who also saw him as a natural captain. He might not be so loud as Watson but he certainly led by example.

Speed must have been thrilled. From playing for the club he supported to scoring for them against arch-rivals Liverpool in front of the Kop, to being named Player of the Year and now the captaincy as well … could it get any better? No, was the unfortunate answer, as the results on the pitch once more took a horrendous turn for the worse. Kendall's third reign proved one step too far; it was an unmitigated disaster, many Everton fans would say. From first game to last, Everton struggled, finishing in 17th place, just one position off relegation. They were only spared that embarrassing fate thanks to a draw with Coventry City on the last day of the season, while main relegation rivals Bolton Wanderers lost at Chelsea. Even then, the two teams each finished on 40 points apiece, with Everton only avoiding relegation because their goal difference (-15) was marginally superior to Bolton's (-20).

By then, Speed had long since left the Merseyside scene, departing at the start of February 1998 in somewhat contentious circumstances, still talked about to this day by Everton fans. As Everton played that tense Goodison Park showdown with Coventry, the man who had begun the season as their captain prepared for a Wembley FA Cup Final appearance with his new club, Newcastle United, and now a teammate of Alan Shearer, rather than in opposition to him.

It was a remarkable sequence of events and there was no sign of the Everton turbulence to come when, an hour before kick-off, Kendall made Speed his captain for the August 9, 1997 opener with Crystal Palace. For Speed it was an immensely proud moment and in that match and beyond, he led his team with dignity despite results caving in around the club. In that Palace game they were defeated 2-1. Indeed, under Kendall's guidance, Everton won just three of their first 18 Premier League matches this time around, with Speed perhaps inevitably scoring in two of those victories, over West Ham and Barnsley, and producing another super show in a 2-0 Merseyside derby triumph over Liverpool. For Everton, that win over the old foe was to be the high spot. As Christmas approached, Kendall's team were in trouble and clearly in need of inspiration. However, Speed helped to provide just that with a last-minute winner away to Leicester and then, after Everton won 3-1 at Crystal Palace to gain some sort of revenge over the Eagles for their opening-day defeat, he was once more on the goal trail as Chelsea were dispatched 3-1 at Goodison

Park on January 18, 1998. Indeed, the far superior Everton could easily have won by a much greater margin that day.

The hat-trick of Speed-inspired victories, coupled with another against Bolton, which he missed and in which Duncan Ferguson belted his own hat-trick, helped Everton climb back up to 14th in the table, from where they eyed brighter days ahead. However, there was a dark cloud looming on the horizon surrounding their new captain and sadly for all parties, Speed would never get to play another game for his beloved side.

Rumours of Newcastle's interest had begun to circulate and a row now ensued over the fact that Speed did not travel on the team coach for a game against West Ham United at Upton Park on the last day of January 1998. It wasn't like him to court unwanted headlines and while Everton earned a commendable enough 2-2 away draw, the travelling blue fans could be heard voicing their disapproval at their absent captain. Ironically, one of Speed's Everton teammates, Slaven Bilić, received an even more hostile reception from the home supporters, having earlier chosen to leave the Hammers for a move to Merseyside.

While Bilić continued to play for Everton for another three years, for Speed the dream was over. By the time the club's next League fixture came around, an away match at Barnsley the following weekend, he was lining up in the famous black and white of Newcastle. Ironically enough, his Toon debut was at St James' Park against West Ham, the very club he had missed playing against, just seven days earlier.

So, why did Speed not travel to London that day? Why did he leave Everton, his boyhood club, so abruptly? What had gone on behind the scenes? Was he dissatisfied with Kendall's management and the poor results the team were achieving? He himself chose to keep his own counsel, telling the *Liverpool Echo*: "I can't explain myself publicly because it would damage the good name of Everton Football Club and I'm not prepared to do that." In fact, he never did explain what had happened.

As a result of his silence, whereby he put the club ahead of his personal feelings and reputation, Speed left himself open to some serious criticism from Everton fans. When he returned to Goodison Park with Newcastle four weeks on, he was roundly jeered whenever he touched the ball. He had never received that sort of vitriolic treatment before as a footballer and while it would never be quite so bad again as that cold February 28 afternoon, he always knew a return to Merseyside as a player in opposing colours would incur some flak.

Despite the condemnation from folk who were his own, namely his fellow Everton fans, Speed continued to maintain what he believed to be a dignified silence. He may have been on the end of a torrent of abuse yet still he had only good things to say about his beloved team in blue. "I never reacted at all to the flak and people can read into that what they like, but it was a privilege and an honour to play for Everton," he insisted, later on in his career. "The only time I'm not an Evertonian is in the 90 minutes I play against them. Everton are a very special club and joining them was the fulfilment of a dream for me. It is special to play for the team you supported as a boy, the team you watched from the terraces – it was a special feeling for me. Being captain was a tremendous honour, too. I will always remember when Howard Kendall told me I would be given the armband – it is something that I could never forget.

"That was a real highlight for me and another was the only hat-trick I ever scored. You get wake-up calls in your career, I suppose, and I got my kick up the backside leaving Leeds to join Everton.

Maybe it had come too easy for me early on. As soon as I got into the team, we won the Division Two title. A couple of years on, we won the League. I would never be disrespectful to Leeds because I love the place, had a great time there, but being in a new environment, with a different viewpoint from people, made me quickly realize I wasn't as good as I thought I was."

After he departed, Everton won just two of their remaining 14 League games, escaped relegation by a whisker and Kendall would soon become another out of the manager's revolving door. Despite the team's clear problems near the foot of the table, his own acrimonious departure and the way the Everton fans had perceived him since then, Speed was a personal success at Goodison Park for a whole host of reasons. He had moved to a new position where he developed his game and took it to new heights. At the same time, he won Player of the Year and in 65 matches scored 18 goals – a fantastic strike rate for any midfield player. In fact, Everton is probably where he had his greatest joy in terms of goals-per-game ratio. Finding the back of the net every three and a bit matches in a team struggling near the foot of the table was no mean feat. Financially, the club didn't do too badly either: Speed was sold to Newcastle for £5.5 million, netting Everton a healthy £2 million profit in the space of just 19 months.

Everton FC, many believed, was Speed's spiritual home and running out before matches to the tune of the *Z-Cars* TV series, the club's pre-match theme song, had the hairs on the back of his neck standing up. For Everton fans, losing their captain at the peak of his powers was hard to take and some argue the sale hurt even more than when England superstar Wayne Rooney, a home-grown Goodison world-class talent in the making, so controversially departed to join Manchester United in a £25.6 million deal in the summer of

2004. Why? Because Gary Speed's departure was a signal that the fallen giants, who with Merseyside neighbours Liverpool had been the dominant force in British football during the previous decade, were much in decline. How many other players of Speed's quality approaching their peak years have Everton subsequently signed? The answer, according to some fans, is zero. That is why Speed's leaving was met with such ferocity. From being kingpins, Everton were now viewed as a selling club. Even in his later years, when he was manager of Wales, Speed readily acknowledged he would come up against some flak whenever he went back to Goodison Park to watch a game. Just eight days before his death, he was attending an Everton v. Wolves Premier League match to run the rule over goalkeeper Wayne Hennessey and midfielder David Edwards, two Welshmen who played for the West Midlands club.

Jokingly or not, Speed talked of perhaps having to go in disguise. These are the words of Barry Horne, a friend and former international teammate, who preceded him as Wales captain. Ironically, Horne himself had to leave Everton as a player upon the arrival at the club of his younger midfield rival: "I was speaking to Gaz before Everton's match against Wolves. I told him I was going to the game and he said he was, too – to check on Edwards and Hennessey. He then said to me, 'I'll probably have to wear a mask!' The fact he felt that way was so sad because he was going to a place where he was the same as everyone else [an Everton fan]."

Horne is a highly intelligent individual who went on to become a football pundit for Sky TV. Thus his opinion on the Speed and Everton issue is well worth noting, particularly given that he is also an Everton fan. "It is a great shame that there was uncertainty and misinformation surrounding Gaz's departure that made things unpleasant," says Horne. "I know Gary left Everton in circumstances which were not ideal and that the fans still do not know the full story behind his departure, but Gary showed dignity in never speaking about it.

"He was selfless, determined, brave; he was intelligent and modest, athletic and the perfect teammate. He was the perfect fit for the club when he arrived and he should have had a long career at Goodison – it was a real shame that it never worked out that way."

Unfortunately, it never did but Speed still left Everton with his head held high. *'Nil satis nisi optimum'* was an appropriate Everton motto in every sense ... for Gary Speed was unquestionably nothing but the best player for them during his all too brief stint at the club he loved.

6

Shearer, Sir Bobby and Great European Nights

"I've waited a long time for this moment and wondered if it would ever come."

Gary Speed – on returning to Champions League football

It takes a special kind of footballer to win the admiration of the Newcastle United supporters. Fanatical fans who appreciate the way the game should be played, they quickly identified Gary Speed's talent and value, and pretty much adopted him as one of their own. For seven years, he pulled on the black-and-white number 11 shirt; for seven years, no one gave more to the Newcastle United cause.

When he joined from Everton for £5.5 million in February 1998, Speed cost just a third of the £15 million British record transfer fee Newcastle had paid to bring Shearer home from Blackburn. Shearer was worth every penny of his high fee because of the flood of goals he scored and the interest and fervour he created. But at his substantially lower price, Speed proved to be an absolute bargain buy. He rarely missed a match, created goals, scored them, made the play, defended his own penalty box, and with Shearer helped the team to three successive top-five Premier League finishes, two Wembley FA Cup Finals and some thrilling UEFA Champions League nights at St James' Park. At one point, Speed was described as being "a rock around which my team is built, a blue chip player". That tribute came from no less a judge than the great Sir Bobby Robson.

Speed was more than just a legendary footballer for Newcastle United on Saturday afternoons, he was also a magnificent ambassador for the club and the city: always engaging, prepared to meet those in the community, consistently creating the right sort of headlines.

Newcastle's genial manager, the club's hierarchy and passionate fans appreciated the positive image that Speed and Shearer projected, because at the time some of the younger team members were capturing banner headlines for all the wrong reasons.

It was up on Tyneside that Speed first got to know Shearer properly and the two older players in the side became the best of mates. On away trips, they roomed together; they holidayed together with their families during the close season, sometimes going away on a yacht in the south of France, where they shared jokes, laughs and a passion to win football matches for Newcastle United. As captains of Wales and England respectively, they brought a wonderful mix of diplomacy, kudos, dignity and playing ability to a Newcastle side looking to recreate the spirit of Kevin Keegan's management years during the mid-1990s.

Under Keegan, and with Shearer to the fore, Newcastle had challenged hard for the Premier League title and wowed the whole of Britain with the adventurous nature of their free-flowing football, although ultimately the superior and more pragmatic spectre of Sir Alex Ferguson's all-conquering Manchester United team loomed large and quashed their dream. Another footballing great, Kenny Dalglish, had replaced Keegan at the helm in January 1997 in a bid to re-energize the team and it was he who signed Speed from Everton on February 6, 1998 as part of that process, giving the new recruit his debut on the very next day.

It was a less than auspicious beginning for Speed, with his new team losing 1-0 at home to West Ham. Shortly afterwards, Speed was to be roundly jeered for the first time in his career when he returned to Everton, the club he had left just 22 days earlier, and found himself on the wrong end of some fearful flak from the Goodison Park faithful. This was uncharted territory, but he maintained a dignified silence throughout and didn't appear to let the criticism affect him, helping Newcastle to a 0-0 draw. As Everton subsequently fought to avoid relegation, he could at least focus on Newcastle's surprise march towards the 1998 FA Cup Final.

Newcastle reached Wembley as a result of a reasonably favourable draw, with Speed helping the Toon overcome Tranmere and Barnsley at home, then Sheffield United at Old Trafford in the semi-finals en route to the final. However, the afternoon of Saturday, May 16, 1998 proved something of an anticlimax when Dalglish's team found themselves outclassed in the final by Arsène Wenger's Gunners. Goals from Marc Overmars and Nicolas Anelka handed Arsenal a comfortable 2-0 triumph; Dalglish reputedly lost a lot of allies that day as a result of Newcastle's lackadaisical display on the big stage. Despite embarking on a multi-million-pound, end-of-season summer spending spree, with German Didi Hamann, Peruvian Nolberto Solano and Frenchman Stéphane Guivarc'h coming on board to bolster the squad, Dalglish parted company with the club after just 12 days and two winless matches into the new 1998–99 season. In his place ventured dreadlocked Dutchman Ruud Gullit, the world's greatest player with AC Milan and Holland towards the end of the 1980s, and whose catchphrase "Sexy Football" was just what the Newcastle fans wanted to hear after the more cautious approach of Dalglish had replaced the thrill-a-minute roller coaster previously enjoyed under Keegan.

With Gullit at the helm, at one point Newcastle reached fifth place in the Premier League table but they had an inconsistent season and finished 13th, although once more the Toon Army booked another date at Wembley. Another more than kind FA Cup draw handed them winnable home ties against Crystal Palace, Bradford, Blackburn and Everton before they edged past Tottenham to reach the final on May 22, 1999 for the second season running.

On this occasion standing in their way were Keegan's old foe Manchester United, heading for the treble of Premier League title, FA Cup and UEFA Champions League crown. Already the League was in the bag and four days after Wembley, Sir Alex Ferguson's side would meet Bayern Munich in that never-to-be-forgotten Euro final in Barcelona, when they snatched a dramatic 2-1 victory, courtesy of injury-time goals from Teddy Sheringham and Ole Gunnar Solskjaer.

Two of Ferguson's key lieutenants, Roy Keane and Paul Scholes, were suspended from that huge showdown with Bayern Munich, the game seen as the Holy Grail by Ferguson. As they were unable to participate in the Champions League confrontation, Wembley was the big final for Keane and Scholes and with wide wizards David Beckham and Ryan Giggs on either side of them in the midfield, they lined up in a much stronger-looking Manchester United team against Newcastle than the one eventually to take the field four days later in Barcelona.

Keane and Scholes were desperately disappointed to be forced out of United's bid to conquer Europe for the first time since the Bobby Charlton and George Best-inspired class of 1968, but vowed to do their bit in the meantime to at least ensure the second part of the treble was suitably secured at Wembley. Keane, the most feared midfield enforcer in Europe and back then at the height of his game, lasted just two minutes of the Wembley clash: injured in a no-holds -barred, blockbusting challenge by Speed, who himself feared no man as he did his bit for the Newcastle cause.

Keane tried to soldier on, but dejectedly had to limp out of the action, his season over. In the Wembley tunnel afterwards, having just held court with the press, he demanded to know of referee Peter Jones (from Leicestershire) why he had not even taken action against Speed for the tackle. In his own autobiography, Keane talked of "seeing Gary Speed another day", but he never did get his own back for that challenge whenever the two midfield rivals met in subsequent matches. Speed was a bit too canny for this. One suspects privately that hard-man Keane may even have had a grudging respect for what Speed did early in battle that afternoon at Wembley. Not that his efforts mattered too much in the end because Newcastle were once more completely outplayed by superior opponents in the final and again found themselves on the wrong end of a 2-0 scoreline. This time Sheringham and Scholes replaced Overmars and Anelka as the match-winning goal scorers.

Two successive trips down to Wembley finished in anguish for the travelling Toon Army, but seeing and hearing almost 40,000 of them outsing the Manchester United hordes that afternoon, even in defeat, merely reinforced Speed's determination to help bring long-awaited success to the Geordie folk. However, those hopes had to be put on hold as a feeling of déjà vu swept over Speed and Newcastle when Gullit departed early on in the following season. He at least lasted 21 days into the new campaign as opposed to the mere 12 days Dalglish had managed the previous season, but was embroiled in conflict with local hero Shearer. There could be only one winner there and Speed knew who that would be, even if Gullit didn't appear to recognize it himself.

Despite Speed scoring in two of the opening four League matches of 1999–2000, Newcastle failed to win any of them and as they approached game number five, a "dare not lose" Tyne and Wear derby clash with north-east rivals Sunderland, intense speculation began to surface about Gullit's future. He responded by taking the biggest (and some would say daftest) gamble of his career, dropping Shearer from the team. It was a move that backfired as Newcastle lost 2-1 to languish just one place off the bottom of the table.

Given Shearer's iconic status among the Toon Army and Newcastle's dreadful start to the campaign, Gullit's position was now clearly untenable. Despite this, the no-nonsense Dutch master refused to backtrack and even revealed he hadn't told Shearer that he was being axed from the starting XI. "It's not about Alan Shearer, it's about Newcastle. And no, I did not tell him personally – the team sheet went up on the board," said Gullit. "We were doing well against Sunderland until we brought Paul Robinson off. We put Alan Shearer on and we lost. What is the conclusion?" That was pretty scathing, but Gullit wasn't finished yet. Later, he would say somewhat harshly of Shearer: "He was England's favourite, England's captain and he was playing for his home town team – all of that meant he was bigger than the club itself. I told him to his face, 'You are the most over-rated player I have ever seen,' but he didn't reply."

Inevitably Gullit departed and so entered the genial 66-year-old grandfather-type figure who was to have such an influence on Speed. Bobby Robson immediately restored Shearer to the starting XI and was rewarded by seeing his new side thrash Sheffield Wednesday 8-0 in his first home match in charge. Shearer bagged a Premier League record five goals in the game; Speed, Kieron Dyer and Aaron Hughes scored the others. Harmony was restored and this was to be Speed's best season for goals as he bagged 13 in total, a record some strikers would have been happy with, let alone a midfielder whose responsibilities also included creating chances for others and stopping the opposition from scoring at the other end of the field.

Speed and Shearer at times proved a deadly attacking combination as they were frequently on the score sheet together, destroying Southampton, Spurs, Bradford and Arsenal that season, as well as netting in that eight-goal rout of Sheffield Wednesday. The bond was growing, as teammates and as friends, and Robson couldn't speak highly enough of his dream duo: "Gary and Alan are the finest role models, on and off the pitch, you can get in football. Shearer's goal record speaks for itself, but Gary is one of the best of the very best as a player. He is totally professional, always gives 100 per cent and has had a fabulous career," he purred. "He is what I call one of my 'blue chip' players, someone I can totally rely upon to produce a consistently high standard of football every single time he goes out onto the pitch. It's not just in matches where Gary shines brightly, he stands out with his effort in training and what he does day in, day out for Newcastle United Football Club. He is a wonderful player to have around this football club. Gary and Alan, in no particular order, are always the very first two names on my team-sheet."

Robson did indeed build his team around the two international captains and he sensed with Shearer and Speed to the fore that Newcastle were on the brink of something very special. The golden era duly arrived in a whirlwind three-year period between 2001 and 2004 when Newcastle briefly went to the Premier League summit, clinched three successive top-five finishes, had great European nights in the UEFA Champions League, reached the semi-finals of the UEFA Cup and wowed the football world once more with the stylish soccer they produced under Robson.

The good times began to roll in the 2001–02 season when, after a bright beginning to the campaign, Newcastle travelled to Arsenal's old Highbury stadium just before Christmas to emerge with a stunning 3-1 victory. They flew back north as Premier League table-toppers and maintained their position looking down on the rest as Speed scored in victories over Middlesbrough and Blackburn, part of a five-match winning sequence that was creating delirium on Tyneside.

One of those five victories was a rip-roaring 4-3 triumph against Speed's former club Leeds United, where the old maestro was named Man of the Match on his return to Elland Road, setting up goals for Wales colleague Craig Bellamy and Robbie Elliott and also winning a penalty kick, which Shearer inevitably converted. "Speed was at the heart of the triumph. At 32, he was like a man reborn," declared the *Guardian* the following Monday.

Fired by the goals of Shearer, the creativity and pace of Bellamy and the midfield orchestration of Speed, Newcastle were still very much in the title hunt as March 2002 approached, but a run of just one win in six matches saw them drop below the big three of Arsenal, Liverpool and Manchester United to finish fourth. Speed missed three of those matches with a rare injury. By the time he returned to the team and helped Newcastle win three and draw one of their last five matches, Robson's team were too far adrift to challenge for the title any longer, although finishing in a UEFA Champions League spot was some consolation at the end of what was still a memorable season.

Speed wasn't quite finished yet, for on May 14, 2002 – a balmy spring evening in Cardiff – he rounded off his best year since Leeds's title-winning campaign a decade earlier by captaining his country to a David versus Goliath 1-0 triumph over Germany at the Millennium Stadium. It was the last match the Germans played before the World Cup finals in Japan and South Korea, when they would march all the way to the final. The goal scored by Wales striker Robert Earnshaw that night would also prove one of only two the Germans conceded in the run-up to that final in Yokohama seven weeks later, when

Ronaldo and Rivaldo beat goalkeeper Oliver Kahn in a 2-0 triumph for Brazil. Post-Earnshaw, and prior to Ronaldo, Ireland's Robbie Keane was the only other person to score against Kahn, his goal coming deep into injury time of a 1-1 draw for Ireland in the World Cup group stages, as the Germans kept otherwise clean sheets in steamrollering their way past Saudi Arabia, Cameroon, Paraguay, the USA and South Korea. Wales's win may have been only a friendly but, for Speed, captaining his country to a win over the World Cup finalists-to-be was yet another impressive addition to his CV.

With Wales having failed to reach the World Cup and Shearer by then retired from England duty, he and Speed were able to go away during the summer, rest their now ageing limbs and come back refreshed for a crack at the UEFA Champions League in 2002–03. It was the first time Speed had played in Europe's top club competition since his involvement with Leeds, 10 years earlier, and he relished what lay in store.

Robson's side were drawn with Italian giants Juventus, crack Ukraine outfit Dynamo Kyiv and UEFA Cup holders Feyenoord in the group stage, prompting Speed to enthuse: "I've waited a long time for this moment and wondered if it would ever come. The Champions League is just so thrilling – when you're sitting at home on a Wednesday night watching television and hear the music come on as the teams walk out of the tunnel, you get butterflies in your stomach.

"I did play in the competition back in 1992 when I was at Leeds, but in those days the first two rounds were knockout ties. We lost to Rangers. In effect, it was over before it started so, in reality, this is my first time at this level. So much happened for me early on in my career that it was easy to think, 'This is what happens in football every year.' It's only when things don't work out that way that you realize maybe you shouldn't have taken everything for granted – I'm going to enjoy these moments."

Enjoy them he did. Given Wales's constant inability to reach the finals of a World Cup or European Championships, and the growing stature and quality of footballer performing in the Champions League, this was as exalted a stage as Speed would get to play on. His manager Robson stated: "I just feel really sorry for Gary – it looks like he is likely to follow in the group of wonderful Welsh players destined not to play in the World Cup and he would really shine at that level. The Champions League is very special, though, and this could be his moment. He is getting better as he gets older. What he has done for me and Newcastle has been phenomenal."

Having breezed through the qualifying round with a 5-0 aggregate victory over the Bosnian minnows FK Zeljeznicar, it is something of an understatement to suggest Newcastle's Euro campaign began poorly at the more important group stage. It was, in fact, horrendous, as they lost 2-0 in Kiev, 1-0 at home to Feyenoord and 2-0 away to Juventus. They were, it appeared, down and out, with any hopes of progress as black as the dark-coloured stripe on Newcastle's shirts. Then commenced one of the most extraordinary turnarounds the competition has ever known. Newcastle provided a glimmer of hope when a goal from Andy Griffin shocked a Juventus side packed with such World Cup aces as Gianluigi Buffon, Alessandro del Piero, Lilian Thuram and Edgar Davids with a 1-0 victory. St James' Park was truly rocking that night, even more so the following week when Speed produced one of his greatest performances in the black and white as he scored the opening goal and then won a penalty (which Shearer nailed) for Newcastle to defeat Dynamo Kyiv 2-1.

Respect and pride had been restored, though progression to the next round still appeared unlikely. Newcastle could do it, however, if they defeated Feyenoord in their final game in Rotterdam and this time it was Speed's Welsh teammate Craig Bellamy who produced his finest performance for the Toon, scoring twice, including the winner deep into injury time, as the Geordie men triumphed 3-2. From being on the brink of extinction, Newcastle had taken nine points from nine to clinch an improbable second place in the group and thus qualification to the next group stage.

Paired this time with Barcelona, Inter Milan and Bayer Leverkusen, it proved a step too far for Robson's team, who were still learning the ropes at this level. They began the second group stage with a 4-1 home defeat by the Italians of Inter and followed that with a 3-1 loss away to Barcelona at the Nou Camp, thus being on the back foot right from the start against two of the genuine powers of the European game. Newcastle did manage to beat Bayer Leverkusen, but another home defeat against Barcelona put paid to any further progress. Defeated, but not disgraced, at least there were once again great European nights at St James' Park and everyone up on Tyneside relished the experience.

So too Speed, although he was now hampered by injuries for the first time in his career and required surgery to cure groin and hernia problems at the beginning of 2003. The exhausting, non-stop sequence of high-pressure Champions League, Premier League and Wales international matches had taken its toll and there was no option but to go under the knife.

"I'm not used to being injured, it's been a frustrating little period for me," he said. Typical of Speed, he wasn't sidelined for long and returned to action in record time to help third-placed Newcastle begin their push for the Premier League title. However, the problem flared up once more when he stretched for the ball while leading Wales to a 4-0 Euro 2004 qualifying victory over Azerbaijan in March 2003 and he wouldn't make another appearance, for club or country, that season. By his standards, Speed missed a large chunk of the campaign yet the facts show he still figured in 41 high-profile matches, more than most could manage.

Of Newcastle's mammoth sequence of 14 Champions League games, Speed appeared in 12 of them. He was still a contender in 24 out of the 38 Premier League encounters as Newcastle finished third, plus five key matches for Wales, who were pushing hard for the Euro finals the following year in Portugal. For Speed, though, that wasn't enough and during the summer he worked harder than ever on his fitness to put injury problems well and truly behind him and build up his strength for what would prove another incredible campaign in 2003–04. That season, you could safely say he made up for lost time, for he featured in no fewer than 61 top-level matches in all competitions – an astounding feat for someone who by that stage was in his 35th year.

Perhaps even more surprising, given his contribution, was the fact that Newcastle appeared to be preparing the ground to introduce competition for the central midfield spots, something Speed must have seen coming after Robson signed Lee Bowyer from West Ham, while young Jermaine Jenas (a £5 million acquisition from Nottingham Forest) broke through to intensify matters. Not that Speed had a problem with the growing battle for places in Robson's starting XI. On the contrary, he relished the new challenge provided by the young guns, for he was still one of them at heart. In terms of age, he might have appeared old for a footballer, but Speed retained the energy, enthusiasm and zip of a younger player and he wasn't ready to stand aside just yet for any emerging new kids on the block.

Explaining his Peter Pan-like approach, Speed declared: "Once you pass 30, you almost have to be fitter than the younger players to compensate for any pace you might lose, that sort of thing. You've got

Above: A young Gary Speed (fifth from the left in the front row) with the Deeside Primary School team for the 1979–80 season. He broke appearance records for the side previously set by Ian Rush before future England star Michael Owen eclipsed his own figures.

Left: Aged 11, Gary Speed (behind trophy) captained the Deeside team which won the Welsh Schools Shield in 1981. Despite being a precocious talent, Speed never earned selection for the Welsh Schools senior team, but he did go on to captain his country at professional level.

Left: One of Speed's earliest Wales appearances, a 5-1 World Cup qualifying defeat against Romania in Bucharest in May 1992. It was the first game of the qualifying campaign, but Wales were to battle back and come close to reaching USA '94, only for a home defeat in their final match to cost them dearly.

Below: Gary (on the right of the front row) celebrates with his teammates in May 1992 after Leeds United clinched the last First Division title before the change to the Premier League era. Among Gary's fellow midfielders are captain Gordon Strachan (two to his left) and Gary McAllister (behind him).

Left: Gary Speed in action for Leeds United in April 1995 during a Premier League match against Newcastle, a club he would later join. Leeds fans regarded Gary Speed as one of their own after he came through the Elland Road ranks and played for them for eight years.

Left: Speed celebrating with teammates Slaven Bilić (No. 28) and Craig Short after an Everton goal against Barnsley in September 1997. Gary grew up supporting Everton and to pull on the famous blue shirt was a dream come true.

Above: Going head to head in the midfield against Manchester United and England's David Beckham in the 1999 FA Cup Final. This was one of two consecutive Wembley FA Cup appearances for Gary in Newcastle colours. Unfortunately, he was to finish on the losing side on both occasions.

Above: England's captain Alan Shearer celebrates a goal with the Wales skipper Gary Speed after Newcastle United find the net against Chelsea in the Premier League in April 2004. Shearer and Speed became close friends on and off the pitch as a result of their time on Tyneside.

Above: Celebrating a last-minute winner from the penalty spot for Bolton Wanderers against Manchester City in September 2005. Speed helped the Trotters push hard to qualify for Europe during his three and a half seasons with the club.

Left: Making his debut for Sheffield United away to Wolverhampton Wanderers on New Year's Day 2008. It was the first time Gary had played a game of football outside the top flight for 18 years, the last occasion having been in an old Second Division title decider for Leeds United in May 1990.

Above: Reaching a major finals with Wales was Gary's unfulfilled dream. Here, he challenges the Ukraine's Andriy Shevchenko in 2001 during a World Cup qualifier at the Millennium Stadium. The game finished 1-1.

Above: The new Wales coach with fellow Welsh and Premier League legend Ryan Giggs during a Wales training session ahead of a Euro 2012 qualifier against England at the Millennium Stadium in March 2011.

Right: Gary on the sidelines during a 2-0 home defeat by England in a Euro 2012 qualifier played in March 2011. It was only his second match in charge of Wales and, in due course, the team was to dramatically improve under their new, progressive manager.

Left: Tributes to Gary Speed left by adoring Leeds fans at the Billy Bremner statue outside Elland Road following the news of his tragic death. He played for Leeds from 1988 to 1996.

Left: Craig Bellamy (No. 8), captain for the night, and regular skipper Aaron Ramsey (in suit) with Edward and Thomas Speed, mascots for the night, at the Wales v. Costa Rica memorial match played on February 29, 2012. It was a highly emotional evening.

Above: Welsh fans hold up red cards bearing the name "Gary" as the two teams lined up for the national anthems ahead of the Wales v. Costa Rica memorial match. That night, at the Cardiff City Stadium, supporters chanted Speed's name throughout the 90 minutes.

to be able to keep up with them. To be fair, in some ways I feel my fitness is better than it was when I was a youngster breaking through at Leeds, simply because I take more care of myself these days. When you're younger, you can eat and drink what you want but everyone who has passed 30 will know that you then start to spread a bit, so you can't overindulge too much.

"I've been lucky with injuries in my career, so to experience what I did last season made it the worst one I have known – I wouldn't want to go through that again. But, rather than rest, I've trained a lot this summer to build up my fitness. I knew I had some ground to make up, couldn't afford to rest on my laurels during the close season. I was coming into the training ground twice a day before the rest of the squad reported, to gain a head start on my fitness.

"There is going to be a lot of competition for places in midfield and that's going to help keep every one of us on our toes. I'm quite pleased with that because I feel we need that extra strength in depth – I certainly don't want us going back to mid-table mediocrity. There's an old saying that you're only as old as you feel and I don't buy this theory that the moment you turn 30, you are on your last legs as a footballer. I'm the fittest player at Newcastle so there can certainly be no excuse for leaving me out of the team because I cannot take the pace.

"Let's just say Alan Shearer and I, who are roommates on away trips, do get a fair amount of ribbing from the younger players about our age. If anything, that provides great motivation. We are two hungry players, who want to show the younger ones we're better than them – which is great for the team because it keeps the youngsters on their toes, as well as us."

Keep them on their toes they did, too, even though Newcastle, once more back in the UEFA Champions League, quickly went out at the qualifying round stage to FK Partizan Belgrade on penalty kicks, the teams having tied at 1-1 on aggregate after the home and away games. A missed penalty once cost Speed qualification for the World Cup finals with Wales, while both Bobby Robson and Alan Shearer had had their share of well-documented misfortune from spot-kick shoot-outs with England. "I guess penalties don't suit any of the three of us," Speed admitted ruefully. "Alan and I were talking about that in the aftermath of the Partizan defeat. If neither of us ever saw a penalty kick again, I think we'd be happy."

To begin with, Newcastle also stuttered in the League, the failure to win any of their opening six matches leaving them down in a lowly and distinctly unhealthy 19th position. They were to recover and eventually finish in fifth spot, but this time around did not represent a serious challenge for the Premier League title and it was a season mainly made memorable for a march that took the team to within one game of the UEFA Cup Final.

At first, Speed was reticent about even being in the competition, knowing Newcastle had been placed in Europe's second-tier tournament because they had failed earlier doors in the Champions League. However, as Holland's NAC Breda, Basle of Switzerland, Norwegians FC Valerenga and Real Mallorca from Spain were one by one swept aside, and a two-legged quarter-final showdown with Dutch giants PSV Eindhoven loomed, Speed and the rest of his Newcastle teammates suddenly found themselves relishing the prospect of European silverware.

"There are lots of massive teams in this competition, including Inter Milan, Barcelona, Celtic, Roma and Valencia. Far from being a sop, we would be delighted to win the thing," asserted Speed. Who then promptly did his bit to put words into actions with another Euro super-show, as PSV came to town for the second leg of their last-eight shoot-out, the first match having finished 1-1 in Eindhoven.

It was already Speed's 52nd match of the season, but there was no sign of him letting up or displaying tiredness as he once more defied age to head home the 69th-minute winner from Laurent Robert's corner in a 2-1 Newcastle triumph at St James' Park on April 14, 2004. The PSV manager was Guus Hiddink, who, on the final whistle, made a point of walking straight over to Speed to warmly shake him by the hand and congratulate him on the 90 minutes of football he had just produced. It was Hiddink's way of displaying appreciation towards Speed, in effect accepting the midfield mastery and artistry the Welshman had displayed was the principal reason his own Dutch side were out of Europe.

"It's very satisfying and my goal has led to more compliments coming my way, but I can't pay too much attention to that. What is more important is that my goal kept us in the hunt for winning the trophy," was Speed's typically modest after-match reaction.

Lying in wait at the semi-final stage were the French side Marseille. It was the first time Newcastle had reached the last four of a European competition since the class of 1969, captained by Bobby Moncur, had won the old Inter Cities Fairs Cup (as it was known back then) 35 years earlier. Expectation was once again high on Tyneside and within the dressing room. Sadly the dream was to end in the semis this time around, with two Didier Drogba goals winning the second leg 2-0 for Marseille in France after the first game at St James' Park finished in a 0-0 stalemate.

That Marseille return clash was Speed's 55th match of the season and he was to pull on the black and white shirt another six times in competitive football, the last occasion coming on May 15, 2004 in a 1-1 draw against Liverpool at Anfield. Shola Ameobi put Newcastle a goal up and although Michael Owen equalized from a Steven Gerrard through ball, the point gained by Newcastle was sufficient to clinch a top-five Premier League finish and thus another crack at the UEFA Cup for the following season.

Despite the intense competition for places as a result of the new young blood being signed by Robson the previous summer, Speed had more than proved he was still good enough for the team. As such he presumed he would be part of the 2004–05 campaign and travelled to the Far East in July 2004, where Newcastle took part in, and won, a pre-season tournament in Hong Kong. While in Asia, though, he learned of negotiations to shift him on to Bolton Wanderers in a £750,000 transfer, a hefty sum for a player fast approaching the start of his 36th year.

Knowing his time to be up, an emotional Speed threw his Hong Kong tournament winner's medal into the crowd, following the final game of the tour. He was departing with a heavy heart and later described leaving Newcastle as "my saddest moment in football". Robson, who in time was to discover and accept that Speed had been sold on too early, also experienced anguish as he bade farewell to his "blue chip" Mr Reliable.

"I could stand here for 10 minutes and talk to you about why Gary Speed will be missed by us, but let me try to sum it up quicker than that by giving him the accolades he deserves," Robson told the press at the time. "That boy will be a miss – he will be a miss in the dressing room, he will be a miss on the pitch, he will be a miss in the tea room, the training ground, the restaurant, the aeroplanes for away trips, the team coach … That boy will be a miss in every concept imaginable for Newcastle United. He is one of my favourites and it is always difficult to let someone like Gary leave. When things have gone badly, he has been the rock people clung onto. When things went well, he was the one who kept others' feet on the ground. Bolton have acquired a very fine player and I wish Gary every bit of luck, happiness and contentment in the world.

"We can't replace Gary Speed – where do you get an experienced player like him, with a left foot and a head?" Robson added, in one of those wonderfully eccentric sayings that he would every now and again come out with during his many years in football. His words were 100 per cent sincere and the compliments were reciprocated as the player said goodbye to Newcastle.

"Sir Bobby was a truly great man-manager. As a player you would've run through a brick wall for him," said Speed. "I learned so much from playing under his management; his football qualities were second to none. It's obviously nice when someone of his stature talks of you in such a nice way and while my move was somewhat sudden, I did have time for a decent chat with him before I left. It was so important for me that I did that.

"I don't know whether it was a difficult decision for Sir Bobby or not. The club have to weigh up the practicalities but I leave with my head held high after what I believe were seven fantastic years. There comes a time in football when you have to move on. That time has come and now I face a fresh challenge. Newcastle United Football Club is not here for the benefit of Gary Speed."

For the record, Speed had appeared in 285 matches for Newcastle, scored 40 goals and was part of a side which went to the top of the Premier League, appeared in Wembley finals and brought truly great European nights back to the area. His biggest achievement, though, was in indelibly making his mark in Newcastle United folklore, even though he wasn't a Geordie.

Mark Jensen, a board member of the Newcastle United Supporters Trust and who publishes a fanzine called *The Mag* (short for 'Magpies'), is perfectly positioned to give the Toon Army's perspective: "When Gary first arrived he was not an instant hit, but we very quickly discovered he was to become a central figure in what developed into a very good team under Bobby Robson. You will always have your one-off players like Alan Shearer, who will stand out as extra-special, but football is about the team – the goal scorer cannot succeed without the team player like Gary.

"He was seen as a model professional. Newcastle didn't always have the best reputation off the pitch at the time because of the actions of some of our younger players, but Speed and Shearer held it all together. They were the steadying influence, on the pitch and off it. I'm not surprised they got on so well – they were cut from same cloth, made of the same type of rock, as such. Those two would be the first ones to come into training, the ones who would do club work out in the community. Bobby Robson called them his 'blue chip' players because they were the ones he could rely upon the most.

"When it comes to Newcastle legends, it obviously helps if you come from the region – the great number nines, like Jackie Milburn and Shearer, will always be right at top of tree, then there are others such as Beardsley and Gazza, who come next. Kevin Keegan and Bobby Robson will forever be revered by us – Bobby was from the area, of course, and while Keegan was born in Doncaster, his family originated from up here. Then, you get the odd individual who breaks into the group because of the way he has played for our club and the way he has behaved off the pitch over a period of time. Shay Given was one of those: adored by the fans, always willing to talk to us, always playing the game in the right spirit. Gary Speed is very much thought of in that ilk, too. They both came from outside the area but they instantly understood what was expected of them, what they were required to give as Newcastle United players, on and off the pitch.

"Newcastle folk are not daft. They may have seen others occasionally give more on the pitch in terms of quality, but certainly not as much as Gary Speed or Shay Given off it. It's not solely about 90 minutes of football. Every day of the week these two were Newcastle United players and were fully aware it mattered what the man on the street thought of them.

"Newcastle is a one-club city and they knew they were representatives of a city, not just a football club. There is a civic thing, not just a sporting factor, with our football club. Footballers these days do get a bad press but there are thoroughly decent ones like Gary, who was always prepared to put himself out. Even after he left us, he often came back to do charity work in Newcastle. He was always prepared to conduct interviews, knowing that was the way you connected with the supporters. He will always be highly thought of by us."

Newcastle – and Robson – missed Gary Speed after he left, dipping down the Premier League table and seeing a return to the bad old days. Barely a month after his departure, Robson himself finished his tenure with the club as a result of a poor start to the 2004-05 Premier League season, saying: "I'm just disappointed I couldn't bring the silverware to the club I wanted to."

As for Speed, he didn't do regrets. He preferred to look forward, emphasizing: "I'm not one for looking back and thinking 'If only'. I left Everton under a cloud as it were and I think it would have been easy for me to have looked back and regretted moving to Newcastle, but while my proudest moment in football was captaining Wales and my happiest was winning the League title with Leeds, my happiest over a period of time was with Newcastle. I loved my time there – the club, the football we played, the city, the people."

Speed was almost certainly a victim of his age, with Newcastle cashing in on someone whose prime years were presumed well behind him. It was somewhat ironic, then, that as he went on to clinch more historic moments in his career under "Big Sam" Allardyce with Bolton Wanderers, Newcastle – the club he left behind – would head downwards in the opposite direction. Far from being washed up, Speed was ready to tackle a new challenge with the Trotters. First off, however, an unfulfilled dream with his homeland was missing from his CV, one that needed to be addressed.

7

14 Years of Heartache

"The high spot of my career, my proudest moment."
Gary Speed – on the honour of captaining Wales

Analyse Gary Speed's glittering career over the best part of two decades and there seems to be next to no room for regrets. He was delighted to have become a League Championship winner with Leeds United and immensely proud to have played for two years with Everton, the club he grew up supporting as a boy. Then the following seven years in front of the fanatical "Toon Army" at Newcastle, where Speed starred in the UEFA Champions League and appeared in two FA Cup Finals at Wembley, turned out to be the happiest spell of his career.

Even his stint at the smaller clubs, the four years with Bolton and two with Sheffield United, would prove enriching experiences. Speed helped Bolton punch way above their weight in the Premier League, while it was at Bramall Lane that he was given his first coaching and then management breaks. But speak to him privately and he would tell you that despite the seemingly non-stop heady days, nights and record-breaking achievements at club level, he was left with one unfulfilled dream: the opportunity, or rather the lack of it, to play for his country in the finals of a major international tournament.

Wales meant everything to Speed and his team's constant failure to clinch a place among the elite hurt him deeply. There was a strong argument for saying that Wales, more than any other nation, were punching below their weight at the top level, given that they had produced international-class footballers of the calibre of Ian Rush, Mark Hughes, Neville Southall, Kevin Ratcliffe, Ryan Giggs, Craig

Bellamy and Speed himself during the 1980s and 90s. Then there were others who also excelled on that stage, such as Dean Saunders, John Hartson, Simon Davies, Mark Delaney, Robbie Savage and Danny Gabbidon, but it simply wasn't to be when it came to qualification for the World Cup or European Championship.

Northern Ireland, Scotland and the Republic of Ireland, who all managed to reach the finals of major tournaments, would have been delighted to include footballers of the quality possessed by Wales, but while each of them enjoyed their respective moments of glory, for Wales it was just heartache followed by more heartache. Speed's longevity as a player meant that he personally had four cracks at reaching a World Cup finals and a further four attempts to get to a European Championship. On two occasions he came excruciatingly close, only for the dream to each time fade away in the most agonizing of fashions.

It was on a scorching-hot Sunday afternoon in Cardiff that Speed was to make his Wales debut, coming on as a second-half substitute in a 1-0 friendly international win over Costa Rica at Ninian Park on May 20, 1990. Speed, who was just beginning to make his mark as a fresh-faced youngster with Leeds United, was selected by then Wales boss Terry Yorath just 24 hours after he had appeared in a Welsh under-21 match, staged a few miles up the A470 dual carriageway in Merthyr Tydfil. To this day, Yorath (himself a former League Championship winner at Elland Road) recalls the moment when he called Speed into the squad. "We had had a couple of late withdrawals through injury and, having seen Gary play a few times for Leeds, I decided he might as well come into the senior set-up," says Yorath. "Gary had played 90 minutes for the under-21s just the day before, but he was young enough and fresh enough to play at least some part against Costa Rica as well.

"In those days we stayed at a hotel called the Country Court on the outskirts of Newport and I still remember the morning Gary bounded into reception – fresh, smiling, happy. Just like the Gary Speed I always knew. I wouldn't say he was completely confident, there was bound to be an element of nerves for any newcomer teaming up for the first time with the big names and big characters we had in our side, but Gary looked the part right from day one. He was well mannered, something which comes from the excellent upbringing he was given by his parents, and quietly spoken. There were other youngsters in the squad at the time who were far more boisterous and outgoing than Gary, but there was just an aura about him which was to hold him in good stead for the rest of his Wales career.

"International footballers always try to find you out, whether that be your teammates who want to test you in training to see if you really have the technical ability to play with them at that level, or the opposition, who tend to be worldly-wise, experienced and look for every trick in the book to get themselves an edge. But our senior players took to Gary straight away – they could see he was the real deal and belonged at that level of football. The opposition quickly discovered that, too.

"I could tell, pretty much from the first time I saw him, that Gary was going to have a long career ahead of him, with club and country. In all my years in football, Gary looked after himself off the pitch as well as anybody else I have seen. Look, he wasn't a Ryan Giggs, Mark Hughes or Ian Rush – the sorts of individual who would stand out on the pitch and invariably capture the back-page headlines with their deeds – but every team needs a Gary Speed, a players' player. He would turn up for every single match, offer nothing less than 100 per cent in every one of those games and produce a consistent level of performance that few could come close to matching. He was a manager's dream, to be honest.

"Gary was never the sort of individual who sought the limelight. In the time I managed him, there was not one single off-the-field occasion when I had to think to myself, 'What on earth has he gone and done that for?' There are quite a few managers who have had that sort of experience with their players down the years but not with Gary Speed. He was a model professional and he was a damn good footballer with it, too. He possessed a terrific left foot, wasn't bad with his right, could score goals, his work-rate was phenomenal and his ability to spring in the air and head the ball with power was as good as that of any centre-forward. After that first late call-up against Costa Rica, it was never a question of whether Gary would be in my squad. He was a certainty from that day onwards, one of the first names I always pencilled in."

Wales's winning goal in that Speed debut was scored by Dean Saunders, who recalls: "Terry had told us on the day of the game that a young lad would be playing, even though he had also appeared for the under-21 side just 24 hours earlier. I didn't know anything about him, but the first impressions were good – he could play all right. I was still relatively new to the Welsh scene myself at the time and I struck it off with Gary straight away. We became quite close and went on to room together for many years after that.

"I remember how, before he went to bed in the evening, Gary would suddenly get down on the floor and do a set number of sit-ups or other exercises, and then demanded I did them too. In time, he went on to break my record of 75 caps for a Wales outfield player and always used to pull my leg about how he was going to do it. He did it, though, and it came as no surprise to me: he was a very special player for Wales."

Four months after Costa Rica, Speed made his full debut for Wales when he started in a 1-0 friendly loss against Denmark in

Copenhagen. Yorath continued to try and ease him in as gently as he could, but Speed was now playing so well it was almost impossible for the manager not to name him in his starting XI. Indeed, Welsh international football was on the up and in the space of three months in 1991, Speed was part of a team that achieved perhaps the greatest back-to-back results in the nation's history. On June 5, Yorath's side rounded off the 1990–91 season with a home European Championship qualifying match against Germany, which boasted an array of stars who had won the World Cup the previous year by defeating Argentina in the final of Italia '90, previously having beaten England on penalties in the semi-finals.

World champions or not, the Germans were that day sent packing from Cardiff with their tails firmly between their legs, Ian Rush's second-half winner giving Wales a never-to-be forgotten triumph. Still buoyed up by events in June, Wales reassembled in September for the first international match of the following campaign, 1991–92. This time footballing aristocrats Brazil, among them star names of the game such as Bebeto, Cafu, Careca, Taffarel and Mauro Silva, were visiting Cardiff Arms Park. The result was the same, though: 1-0 to Wales, thanks to a Saunders goal, which Speed helped set up. Another giant of the world game was defeated by the resurgent Wales.

Speed had arrived on the international stage and from that point, he was a fairly permanent fixture in the starting line-up. There were further highs under Yorath's management, including another never-to-be-forgotten Arms Park game, this time a World Cup qualifier against Belgium on March 31, 1993, when a new 18-year-old sensation called Ryan Giggs burst onto the scene with his full debut.

Giggs had already made his Wales bow a year and a half earlier when he came on as a late substitute in a 4-1 thrashing by Germany in Nuremberg. His first start for his country culminated in a breathtaking debut goal from an unstoppable free kick, which flew over the defensive wall and into the Belgian net. In unison the Welsh crowd began chanting "Ryan Giggs, Ryan Giggs, Ryan Giggs". A new sporting superstar had been born and already the pundits were predicting Giggs could eclipse Rugby Union scrum-half legend Gareth Edwards as the finest sportsman Wales had ever produced. Wales eventually won the game 2-0 and, Speed hoped, had taken a gigantic step towards USA '94.

Suddenly, the two new glamour stars of British football were together in Yorath's squad. Speed was already wowing the girls with his youthful looks and graceful footballing ability, but even he was eclipsed by Giggs. In those days, Giggs, one of the leading teen heart-throbs, was receiving 3,000 fan mail letters a week. With the two young players turning heads the moment they walked into a room, for Wales, they were a marketing dream.

Together the two would go on to share a roller-coaster ride of incredible highs and demoralizing lows, as well as a lifelong friendship. In a way, it might be said that Giggs looked up to Speed (senior by four years), if not as a mentor, then certainly as the kind of teammate anyone would be proud to line up with. Later, in 2011, when Speed became manager of Wales, he attempted to persuade Giggs to come on board as a coach (effectively to groom him to one day become his successor). Although the two men went on to have conversations about the role, the move never did materialize, as Giggs chose to continue concentrating upon the demands of his playing career at the top level with Manchester United.

Back in 1993, Ryan Giggs and Gary Speed represented the playing future for Wales and, side by side, they would line up for their country for another decade. However, the Manchester United and Welsh legend once declared unequivocally that Speed was Wales's most important player, a far more valuable contributor to the cause than himself. "Gary is the one player you want to see lining up for the anthems every time we play; he is such an important influence on the team," stressed Giggs. "So much of what he does, on and off the pitch, goes unheralded, but we would not be the team we are without him. His calming influence rubs off on everyone and he gives us all the confidence to play our own game. The team looks a little bit lost when Gary is not playing – we are a different team when he plays."

Praise indeed, but Giggs meant it and six months after his own full debut wonder-show against Belgium, he and Speed were to line up next to one another again when Romania visited the Arms Park on November 17, 1993. Clearly they would not know it at the time, being as young as they were, but this game would prove the most important match of either man's international career.

Victory for Wales would have enabled the Dragons to reach the World Cup in the United States the following summer. Anything less and the hard-nosed, tough-tackling Romanians, who mixed rugged tactics with wonderful flair from their playmaker captain Gheorghe Hagi, would go through. It was classic win-or-bust for Wales and a capacity crowd settled into their Arms Park seats to witness one of the most nerve-jangling, nail-biting 90 minutes any football fan has ever known. That Wednesday evening, there was enormous expectation on the shoulders of Giggs, Speed, Ian Rush and Wales's other stars – the weight of an entire nation, in fact – and perhaps predictably the occasion got the better of them early on.

Romania took a 32nd-minute lead when Neville Southall, whose brilliance between the sticks for Wales and Everton had made him the world's number one goalkeeper, inexplicably and uncharacteristically allowed a long-range shot from Hagi to dip under his body and go into the Welsh net. The fantastic passion and fervour displayed by the Welsh crowd up until that point suddenly turned into silence. At half-time, Wales went in with their heads down and spirits flagging, but typically it was Speed who led a dramatic turnaround in second-half fortunes. In the 60th minute he rose splendidly above giant Romanian defenders to head a Giggs free kick towards goal and Dean Saunders touched the ball home from close range.

Cue hope and some distinctly rattled Romanians. One more goal and Wales, by now the better team, were through. Barely 60 seconds later, and before the Romanians could recover from the Welsh goal, the irrepressible Speed once more advanced into the Romanian penalty box, where he was bundled over in the challenge by Dan Petrescu. Swiss referee Kurt Rothlisberger immediately pointed to the penalty spot.

Inside the ground there was pandemonium, bedlam, confusion and sheer joy: for Wales, this was the moment. Left-back Paul Bodin, of little Swindon Town, was tasked with taking the high-pressure penalty. Though certainly not one of Wales's more high-profile players and lacking the stardust of a Giggs, Saunders, Speed or Rush, Bodin had scored from the spot in the previous game and established himself as deadly from 12 yards out … until this particular moment, the most important of all. Bodin crashed his shot against the crossbar and so Romania escaped. Five minutes from time, Florin Răducioiu scored the winner and there was heartbreak for Speed, Giggs and the rest of the Welsh team. Had Bodin converted the penalty, he would have sent the Dragons through to the 1994 World Cup in the United States as Britain's only representatives and the sporting landscape in the principality would have changed forever. What started out as an evening of hope and expectation now turned into anguish and utter despair.

Yorath, the Wales's manager that night, today recounts how fate altered the course of events and so nearly set up a Welsh World Cup appearance which, with the rugby team struggling at the time, many believe could have permanently altered the way that the two sports are perceived in Wales: "Midway through the second half, when we were losing 1-0, I turned to Peter Shreeves, my assistant in the dugout, and said I wanted to bring on a substitute. The plan was to take Bodin off, push Gary Speed back to left-back and place Jeremy Goss in his position in the midfield. We were definitely going to make the switch but suddenly we started to get on top for the first time and Gary helped us get that equalizing goal. Before we had finished celebrating ourselves and had a chance to take stock, Gary won that penalty as well. It all happened so quick.

"If Bodin had been taken off – as was my plan, just a couple of minutes before – Gary, or perhaps Dean Saunders, would have been told to take the penalty. Probably scored, too. I have often wondered to myself over the years what might have happened had I gone through with that substitution as I had intended. Anyone can miss a penalty and no one blames Paul for what happened that night, but I did note the irony three days later when, travelling home from a match in Manchester, I turned on the car radio and discovered Bodin had scored a penalty for Swindon that day. Unbelievable!

"Gary would have lit up the world stage, had we got to the World Cup. He was just one of those players who would never have shirked responsibility or become overawed by the sense of occasion. Some leading players just don't do it on the big stage – for evidence of that, just look at England in the World Cup finals in South Africa in 2010. Gary would have been fine, make no mistake about that.

"The dressing room was very quiet after the match and there wasn't much I could say to console the players, particularly the more senior ones like Rush and Southall. I remember when I was playing and we lost a win-or-bust qualifier against Scotland in 1978. I knew afterwards that was it, my last chance of appearing in the World Cup had gone. Ian and Nev knew time was up for them, too, but the younger ones, like Gary and Ryan, would never have imagined this would prove to be as close as they ever got. No one would have envisaged that."

So near and yet so far, afterwards the senior players in the team were inconsolable: they knew this had been their big chance. For Speed, now 23, and the 19-year-old Giggs, however, it was assumed there would be plenty more opportunities.

As manager, Yorath was able to keep some sort of perspective on the defeat because he himself had lost a son and following this tragic event, he knew that football, however important, was ultimately only a game. A year before the Romania game, 15-year-old Daniel Yorath had died after collapsing with a heart condition while kicking a ball about in the back garden of the family home with his dad. Daniel had been a promising footballer and, like Speed, had just signed schoolboy forms with Leeds – "He was a great lad and was very keen to make it as a footballer," says Yorath.

Just days after the Romania defeat, and much to the chagrin of many Welsh players and the majority of the fans, Yorath was summarily dismissed by the FA of Wales. Many Welsh players went public in voicing their disquiet at the decision but Speed, ever the diplomat, chose to keep his own counsel even though he was close to Yorath and always grateful to him for providing his international break. Over the course of the next six years, a period of uncertainty and sporadic results ensued. It was a fallow time, which privately infuriated Speed – he had come so close to the dream against Romania and could not understand why Wales were no longer in the ball park.

However, he did enjoy the high of scoring his first goal for Wales in a European Championship qualifier against Moldova in Kishinev on October 12, 1994, but it was in defeat as the team now managed by likeable Englishman Mike Smith surprisingly lost 3-2.

Smith had done a magnificent job for Wales during a previous spell as manager during the 1970s, but two decades on many believed he was now out of touch with modern-day football at the elite level. A 5-0 defeat in Georgia the following month, one of Speed's low points with Wales, merely reinforced that view. Just a year or so after Yorath had been dismissed, Smith too appeared to be fighting for his job and for a game against Bulgaria in Cardiff at the end of 1994 he tried to pull off what he believed to be a masterstroke: finding Welsh ancestry in one Vincent "Vinnie" Peter Jones. The English football hard man would later star in the Hollywood movies *Lock, Stock and Two Smoking Barrels* (1998) and *Gone in Sixty Seconds* (2000).

Back in his football playing days, Vinnie was an enforcer of a midfield player with a Wimbledon team dubbed the "Crazy Gang". One of his claims to fame was an infamous photograph of him trying put Paul Gascoigne off his game by grabbing him by the testicles during a Dons versus Newcastle FA Cup match in 1988. Born in Watford, England, and with a broad London accent, extrovert Vinnie had somehow dug up a few Welsh roots from Ruthin, near Wrexham. The paperwork having been supplied to FIFA, Smith immediately selected him for his team in the must-win clash with the Bulgarians. There were suggestions from some that this was a publicity stunt to boost flagging Wales crowds: Vinnie had a red Welsh dragon tattooed above his heart and there were plenty of comments made as to his suitability for this level of the game. Legendary TV pundit and former England striker Jimmy

Greaves got in on the act: "Well, stone me! Just when you thought there were truly no surprises left in football, Vinnie Jones turns out to be an international player."

However, Speed, who knew Jones from his Leeds United days, was not so dismissive of his new international teammate and welcomed him into the fold as they became unlikely compatriots in the midfield. Not that this was to much avail, for Wales lost the game 3-0. Six months later Smith was gone, to be replaced by Bobby Gould for the next part of Speed's playing years for Wales.

Like Vinnie Jones, Gould's main claim to fame had been with Wimbledon, where as manager he helped the south London side shock Kenny Dalglish's star-studded Liverpool to win the FA Cup in one of Wembley's greatest-ever contests, back in 1988. Full of charisma, charm and effervescence, Gould breezed into the Wales job. His PR skills also won over the Welsh media (whom he cleverly kept onside during his reign) when he arranged a 30-minute match for them against Speed and the rest of the team at Cardiff Arms Park. For the Welsh press – most of whom were, naturally, frustrated would-be footballers – this was the game of their lives. Quite what finely toned Premier League footballers such as Giggs and Speed made of facing a bunch of amateurs is not so certain.

Whatever, the match duly took place on a Monday lunchtime on October 9, 1995, 48 hours before Speed, Giggs et al. were due to take on Germany at the same Arms Park venue in another big European Championship qualifier. Afterwards, the manager revealed that he even changed his planned starting XI against the Germans as a result of what he had seen in the knockabout against the scratch press team, with Geraint Williams dropping out and Nathan Blake coming in. Williams probably never lived that one down, but that was Bobby Gould for you – enigmatic, different, prepared to do things his way. Like Smith, he was perhaps out of his depth in the Wales job, although you couldn't help but like him.

Fortunately Speed did not lose his place as a result of that kick-about. For the record he forced an own goal from a corner in a 3-0 win over the Welsh Press XI (Ryan Giggs and Dean Saunders netted legitimately and we media lads were unable to get remotely near the penalty box of a clearly bored Neville Southall). The following season, part of Speed may have been secretly wishing he had indeed been dropped when Wales travelled to Eindhoven to meet Holland in a World Cup qualifying game.

Eindhoven: a name which sends shivers down the spine of any Welsh football fan. The date in question was November 9, 1996 and it must surely rank as the worst defeat of Gary Speed's career. Gould's regular skipper Barry Horne was missing that night and before the game the manager surprisingly conducted a secret ballot among those players present asking who they wanted as captain. Vinnie Jones edged it with three votes and so, less than two years after coming on board with Wales, he was now wearing the captain's armband, too. Speed (who received two votes) came second.

Vinnie had been part of a Wimbledon team that had forged a reputation, shall we say, for brawn and route-one football rather than the aesthetic way they played the beautiful game. As Wales captain for the day against a star-studded Dutch team consisting of Dennis Bergkamp and a number of other leading lights who would go on to reach the semi-finals of the World Cup in France '98, Vinnie delivered a rousing pre-match message in a television interview aired shortly before kick-off. "Well, we've gotta give it some!" he thundered (in footballing parlance, don't be overawed, get stuck into the tackles, rattle the Dutch and stop them from producing their breathtaking, free-flowing football). It was similar to the way the Wimbledon of old so often succeeded against stronger opposition.

For 22 minutes the Welsh spirit prevailed, although the scoreline remained 0-0 because of the brilliance of Neville Southall, who, even by his own lofty standards, had perhaps the game of his Wales career in goal, pulling off wave upon wave of superb stops. Then, after 22 minutes, Bergkamp finally beat "Big Nev" to open the scoring. The final result was Holland 7, Wales 1 and if not for Southall, it would have been 20.

From that point on, Gould determined a change of plan was needed. Vinnie was not exactly gone in 60 seconds, but shortly afterwards he was pretty much history and the following spring – May 27, 1997 – Speed was for the first time handed the captaincy of Wales. He was to retain the armband for the rest of his Wales-playing days, a record 44 times in total. Of those 44 internationals, Wales duly won 13, drew 12 and lost 19.

The game in which he made his captaincy bow was a friendly international against Scotland in the unlikely setting of Kilmarnock's Rugby Park and Speed got off to a flier as Wales triumphed 1-0, courtesy of a John Hartson goal. Recalling the moment, Gould says: "Gary just seemed a natural leader to me but let me tell a little story here. Barry Horne, who had been Wales's captain for a number of years, wasn't in the squad any more and my first choice to replace him was Mark Hughes. I approached Sparky and told him, 'We need to move on, I'm looking to make you Wales's captain.'

"He replied, 'With all due respect, Bob, I think you should go and speak to Gary Speed first. He is the more logical choice for me.' Gary, I was told, believed he was the next in line and as I thought about what Mark had said, it made clear sense. Mark was our target man, a goal-scorer, and in that sort of position you need to be selfish.

As a midfield player, linking all areas of the team, Gary was clearly the more obvious choice to take responsibility for the whole side.

"I went to see him in his room to tell him the good news. 'What took you so long?' was his first reaction, although I must emphasize it was said with a big grin on his face. After that we struck up a rapport and I went to visit him on several occasions to discuss the Wales team and the way we should go forward. I'm a great believer that you need to have played international football to be a manager at that level, because the demands of the game are so different. I had never played at that level and Gary could notice my limitations. He tried to help me out, give me an understanding of where the players were coming from, what their point of view was."

Gould himself admits it wasn't always a friendly eye-to-eye conversation and there were occasions when he and Speed would exchange angry words, although he again stresses the captain only spoke up because he felt so passionately about Wales and desperately wanted them to win. One of their main bust-ups came in the dressing room, in front of all the other players, immediately after Wales had been thumped 4-0 by Tunisia in Tunis. It was an end-of-season friendly international in June 1998. Gould had plucked a teenage defender nobody had ever heard of called Ryan Green from Wolverhampton Wanderers and, three days earlier, handed him his Wales debut in a 3-0 win over Malta. In doing so, Green (aged 17 years and 226 days) eclipsed the great Ryan Giggs as the youngest-ever player to be capped by Wales, a record subsequently overtaken by Gareth Bale in 2006.

Giggs himself once described the move as something of a gimmick, but having picked Green against Malta, Gould gave the kid from Cardiff another chance against Tunisia, in addition to other young players. But the move backfired as Wales were battered 4-0 and Gould admits Speed let him know exactly what he thought.

"Gary had no axe to grind with any individual player but we did have a confrontation that day," he recalls. "The trip hadn't started well because we pitched up in what we all thought was a right poxy hotel. As captain he said to me, 'We're not having this,' so I told him to keep the lads happy for a while as I went searching for a better hotel. We ended up with a beautiful place but his mood hadn't been great because he felt, quite rightly, the Wales international team deserved a more appropriate base than the one they had originally been given.

"Gary wasn't too pleased afterwards either when I told him I needed to experiment for this game and pick the younger players. I had to look to the future, I explained. He was there to win for his country, he replied, and let's just say we had to agree to disagree. After we had lost so heavily he let me know exactly what he thought of my team selection, but it was never done with malice and I never took offence. Gary was simply fighting the corner for Wales, which meant so much to him. I was of the school of thought that if someone had a point of view they felt strongly about, let him get it off his chest and we move on. We exchanged sharp words that day but only because Gary was so desperate for Wales to succeed.

"I never held the row against him. International management is entirely different to club management. Without the day-to-day involvement, it can be a lonely existence. Gary didn't agree with some of my footballing principles or tactics and knew I was short of knowledge at that level – that is why he tried so hard to help, to let me know, as a senior player, that he believed we should be doing certain things in a different way. Do you know, I learned so much from Gary Speed and would do the job in a completely different way today, were I to have my chance again. That time we spent together created something of a bond between us and when Gary went on to become Wales manager himself, I would call him now and again and say, 'Well done.' I think he appreciated that support, just like I appreciated his support of me when he was my captain."

A year down the line, Speed, Gould and Wales were on the end of another 4-0 battering, this time by Italy in Bologna on June 5, 1999. Deep into the Italian night the manager announced he was quitting the job because he felt he could take the team no further. At half-time, Gould had ripped into his strikers, Ryan Giggs and Dean Saunders, pointing out that they were not showing for the ball and were letting down their teammates. At the end of the match he told them that he was quitting. In his autobiography, Giggs quipped that if he and Deano had known it was that simple beforehand, they might have done so in previous matches, too!

Cue the arrival of Mark Hughes as Wales manager in the autumn of 1999 and the start of a truly incredible up-and-down spell for the team of boom or bust, with very little in between. Having turned down the honour of the captaincy himself under Gould, by saying Speed was a better choice, it made sense that Gary would keep the armband under Hughes. What followed was an incredibly close relationship with his manager, with Speed acting as Hughes's eyes and ears and his trusted lieutenant on the pitch.

Hughes, who was brought up with the best facilities as a Manchester United footballer, detested the Ragbag Rovers image that he believed the Welsh team possessed and so he went about forcibly changing the way the side approached matches. They were now given the very best hotels and proper training facilities, chartered planes for away matches (rather than having to travel with the public) and were handed a huge team of masseurs, nutritionists and others to help out behind the scenes.

"Players always look for excuses. Take any excuse away in terms of how we prepare for matches and they are likely to perform better on the pitch," explained Hughes.

Speed loved the new set-up and, as captain, went public by saying: "This is just brilliant. Sparky should be given a contract for the next 10 years, because Welsh football is definitely going in the right direction and we need to ensure that continues. I'm really optimistic about the future for Wales."

Hughes's debut game, a match in Belarus on September 4, 1999, was marked by Speed with the first goal of the new era as Wales triumphed 2-1, Giggs grabbing the winner. The team then moved to the newly built Millennium Stadium in Cardiff, where unheard-of attendances began to follow the players. The first football match played at the ground was on March 29, 2000, a meaningless friendly against Finland, and the FA of Wales chose to pitch ticket prices at £5 for adults and £3 for children, hoping the low prices would at least attract around 10,000. Sporting crowds had to be phased gradually into the new ground because of health and safety issues, so the capacity for that game was pitched at 66,000, rather than the customary 74,000. Within 48 hours, every single ticket had been snapped up. Speed and his teammates were stunned: it was incredible. To put the figure into context, it is worth pointing out that barely 5,000 hardy souls had bothered to turn up for Wales's previous home match, a nondescript 2-0 European Championship qualifying defeat against Switzerland, staged at Wrexham's Racecourse ground. Two months after the Finland sell-out, 74,000 turned up at the now full-capacity Millennium Stadium to watch another friendly international, this time against Brazil.

For a golden 18-month period, with Speed as captain, little old Wales became the best-supported side in Europe. Yes, even better than traditional super powers England, Italy, Spain and Germany, as the Millennium Stadium was regularly packed to capacity. So much for Rugby Union being the only sport the people want to follow in Wales. A potent mix of cheap ticket prices, pitched by the Football Association of Wales as low as £3 and £5, the newly built Millennium Stadium, the fresh iconic symbol of Wales at the start of the 21st century which everybody wanted to see, and the fact that the side captained by Speed suddenly started to win matches led to unprecedented support for the national team. The high spot, Speed himself acknowledged, came on March 29, 2003, when an incredible 74,000 crammed into the Millennium on a sunny Saturday afternoon to watch Wales take on Azerbaijan.

"Seeing the sea of red around the stadium lifted us all," recalled Speed. "We weren't playing one of the super powers, were we, but Azerbaijan. It was incredible. We couldn't let the fans down." They didn't either: Speed inevitably put his words into action by leading from the front and scoring himself early on as Hughes's team thumped the Azeribaijanis 4-0. Yes, the fans went home happy that day.

There was much pain to go through, however, before the dawning of what seemed a golden age for Speed and Wales for the first time since the ill-fated bid to reach the World Cup under Yorath. The crowds were coming to the Millennium Stadium, yet that Finland match, which was incidentally lost 2-1, was the start of a record run of 12 matches without a win. As well as Finland, Wales lost to Brazil (0-3) and then also failed to beat Portugal, Belarus, Norway (twice), Poland (twice), Armenia (twice) and Ukraine (twice). It was the worst run of results since the team managed by Dave Bowen between 1968 and 1970 also went 12 matches without a win, and had Hughes's Wales failed to beat Belarus in an otherwise meaningless end of the World Cup campaign qualifier in Cardiff on October 6, 2001, the team skippered by Speed would have entered the annals of fame on their own for all the wrong reasons.

Media headlines beforehand posed questions such as 'WALES'S WORST ... OR ARE THEY?' The facts and figures were presented and serious questions asked as to how a side containing the likes of Giggs, Speed, Craig Bellamy and John Hartson could possibly be ranked as the worst in history. The media demanded that they begin winning matches under Hughes ... and fast. But Hughes didn't take kindly to the way the agenda had been set ahead of the game, with further headlines such as 'SPARKY'S WALES FACE HUMILIATION' in subsequent days and he rapped: "It's ridiculous! I have played in far worse Welsh teams than this one, I can assure you of that."

Speed, who was playing for Newcastle at the time, was oblivious to the stories until he got to Wales. "I know nothing about this, but I think we all need to calm down a bit and it's up to us players to beat Belarus and put an end to this talk of unwanted records," he said in typically understated style.

In the event Wales did win the match 1-0 and the result kick-started the most glorious two-year period of Speed's international career. From being joint worst, the team now embarked on a run which saw them enter the record books for entirely different reasons. This time they went on a run of nine matches without defeat, ovetaking the previous best figure of eight held jointly by the Wales's team which reached the 1958 World Cup under Jimmy Murphy and the class of the early 1980s managed by Mike England.

From the worst to the best, those were truly heady days. Speed was captain of a Wales team that defeated Italy (2-1) and Germany (1-0) at the Millennium Stadium, drew with Argentina (1-1) and the Czech Republic (0-0), and also beat Finland and Azerbaijan (twice).

Throw in a draw with Bosnia and that opening win over Belarus and it became the never-to-be-forgotten nine. The run of results included victories in the opening four matches of Wales's bid to reach Euro 2004 in Portugal, a feat matched elsewhere in Europe at the time only by reigning champions France, which had world greats such as Zinedine Zidane, Thierry Henry and Marcel Desailly inspiring them. Being ranked with the French took Welsh football to new heights and there were regular sell-out crowds at the Millennium. A new-found buzz was created until, as always seemed to happen with Wales, fate took an unfortunate hand.

On March 29, 2003, Speed had scored and led his side to a 4-0 Euro-qualifying win over Azerbaijan, a result which gave them the maximum points haul of 12 out of 12. Confidence among Speed and his teammates was at an all-time high: the players were ready and willing to take on anybody and were firmly of the belief that they would win, whoever the opposition, wherever the match. Next up, just four days later, they were due to play Serbia and Montenegro in Belgrade and were fully anticipating that they would make it 15 points out of 15 and go another step closer to the finals in Portugal the following year. Speed was all set to travel. However, news had emerged of the assassination of Serbian Prime Minister Zoran Djindjic on March 12, 2003. A state of emergency was declared and the match had to be postponed for security reasons. "The Serbian government do not want any sporting event in the city or surrounding area," said UEFA director of communications and public affairs Mike Lee. "Therefore it was appropriate to postpone the game, and the two associations and UEFA have agreed on a new date."

That rescheduled fixture eventually took place on August 20, 2003. However, the momentum Wales had so splendidly built up had unfortunately disappeared. Even within the still relatively short space of time before it took place the wheels had begun to come off. Hughes arranged an end-of-season friendly against the USA in California in May, but no fewer than 17 of his players didn't know the way to San Jose, or so it seemed, and pulled out of the game for a variety of reasons. Speed was injured, having undergone surgery for a hernia problem, yet he still turned up and travelled to the States, even though he was unable to play. He wanted to show his support for Hughes, who was clearly in need of a boost after so many withdrawals, and to do whatever he could to aid the squad.

Perhaps predictably, Wales lost to the USA 2-0 and from that moment on, they never seemed to recover under Hughes. They were also defeated 1-0 after travelling to Serbia and Montenegro – the start of another unwanted record run, this time of 10 competitive matches without a win. As a result, they finished the Euro campaign almost as poorly as they had begun it so wonderfully well, with defeats to Italy and Serbia (twice) and a draw with Finland meaning they finished second in the group and had to battle it out with Russia for the right to reach Portugal via the play-offs.

The Finland game in Cardiff on September 10, 2003, which finished 1-1, in fact marked the occasion when Speed overtook Dean Saunders's record as the most capped outfield player for Wales. Predictably he played down his big moment, saying: "I'm obviously proud and will look back on this fondly one day, but what matters most is not me getting a record but Wales winning the match." Sadly, they didn't go on to achieve this and were picked off by Italy for the top spot in their group 4-0. And so they went into the enormous two-legged showdown with Russia in the November of 2003. Speed splendidly led his side to a backs-to-the-wall 0-0 draw in the first leg in Moscow, setting up the Euro 2004 play-off decider in front of a capacity 74,000-capacity crowd at the Millennium Stadium on

November 19. It was the biggest match Speed had played since that Romania World Cup showdown a decade earlier.

This time, as with the senior professionals such as Rush and Southall back in 1993, it was Speed's last opportunity to reach the finals of a European Championship. Again, as with Romania, it was another tight, tense affair and nerves once more got the better of Wales. Many believe manager Hughes was too defensive in his formation that evening and a solitary goal early on from Vadim Evseev condemned Wales to more last-match qualifying misery.

Shortly afterwards a row erupted over Igor Titov testing positive for an illegal performance-enhancing substance called Bromatan-DM following the play-off shoot-out held in Moscow, four days earlier. Wales argued that Titov, who was subsequently banned for a year by world football's governing body FIFA, was ineligible to play in the Cardiff return fixture and therefore they should be awarded the match and, in turn, a place in the finals in Portugal instead of the Russians. Indeed, Wales felt so strongly about the matter that they first appealed to UEFA and then, when the protest was rejected, even took their case to the Court of Arbitration for Sport (CAS) in Lausanne. But the World Anti-Doping Code stated that in the event of one member testing positive for a prohibited substance, it was the individual and not the team who must be held liable. Thus Russia retained their place in Euro 2004, whereas Wales's players went on their summer holidays.

At least on that occasion, as with a decade earlier in the race for USA '94, Speed came within one match of fulfilling what many believed to be his deserved destiny on the biggest football stage of all. He himself didn't say too much about the drugs controversy, but while he would have relished the opportunity to lead his country into the Euro Finals, he gave the impression that he wouldn't have been overly happy doing so via a back-door route. At least he had broken the Welsh cap record for an outfield player and Yorath, the manager who gave him his international debut, says: "Gary went ahead of legendary players who have worn the Welsh shirt down the years. Two words summed him up best: fitness and consistency. He was our Mr Dependable, our Mr Consistency, and would have been very proud of that record."

There was still time for one last attempt at a World Cup: the 2006 tournament in Germany. However, Wales took just two points out of their opening four matches against Azerbaijan (1-1 draw), Northern Ireland (2-2 draw), England (0-2 defeat) and Poland (2-3 defeat). That Poland game, staged on October 13, 2004, proved the end for Hughes as manager and Speed as captain too. Given the close professional relationship the two men had forged, it was perhaps appropriate that they bowed out together.

When Wales were 3-1 down approaching the closing moments Hughes took off Speed, who was given a rapturous ovation by the Millennium Stadium crowd when he bade farewell to the fans. John Toshack, who would eventually succeed Hughes as manager, had hoped that Speed would carry on for another couple of years, believing that his professionalism would rub off on and help bring through the youngsters he had started to pick. But Speed explained his decision to call it a day by saying: "To captain your country is the biggest honour in the game and I'm really proud to have done it on so many occasions, but with so many good youngsters coming through, if I step down and give someone else a go, that must be good for Welsh football.

"I leave having enjoyed every minute of Mark Hughes's time in charge. I learned so much under him. We were down in the dumps, but he lifted us up. I will now become Wales's biggest fan, cheering them on in every game."

Speed finished with a record for Wales which read as follows: played 85, won 29, drew 16, lost 40. The high spots in his playing career (stretching from 1990 to 2004) clearly came with 13 wins from 23 games played under Yorath and 10 victories and 11 draws from 33 matches under Hughes's management. But with the highs and expectation came the lows, and given what was at stake, Romania and Russia were the worst moments of Speed's entire career. Having failed to get there as a player, he determined to right the wrong as a manager and at the tail end of 2011, there was a real buzz about how the young Wales team he was so splendidly leading would be in with a genuine chance of reaching the 2014 World Cup in Brazil.

Don't be misled into believing that Speed's playing career with Wales was a failure, though. On the contrary, he had had a magnificent time and ended up breaking a whole string of records. He won more caps for an outfield player than any other footballer in Wales's history, his final tally of 85 internationals easily eclipsing the next best figure of 75 held by Dean Saunders. Only the great Neville Southall, the legendary Wales and Everton goalkeeper, bettered Speed's tally, appearing 92 times for his country.

Had he been the least bit selfish, Speed could easily have gone on to play another eight matches for his country, which would have enabled him to break the landmark figure set by Big Nev. But, on retiring from international football in October 2004, Speed told confidants in typically modest fashion: "Why should I insult Nev by carrying on just for the sake of breaking his record? Yes, I know I could do it, but he was a true legend of our game and I've no desire whatsoever to cheapen his achievements by playing on just so I can surpass Nev's record. He was one of the greatest footballers Wales has produced and deserves to be our record cap holder. That's the way it's going to stay, as far as I'm concerned."

In any case, there were plenty of other landmarks for Speed. He captained his country a record 44 times, one more game than Terry Yorath and well ahead of Kevin Ratcliffe (37 matches as skipper), Barry Horne (33 matches) and Ryan Giggs (18 games).

He came so close to the dream, but although it remained unfulfilled it's fair to say that few played for Wales with more passion, pride and commitment than Gary Andrew Speed. Reflecting on being given the Wales captaincy, he smiled and said: "The high spot of my career, my proudest moment."

8

Renaissance at the Reebok

"It makes me feel old whenever people mention this record! I'm just out to keep playing."

Gary Speed

Having left high-flying Newcastle United, with Bobby Robson's team finishing fourth, third and fifth in successive Premiership seasons and also featuring in the UEFA Champions League, the natural assumption was that the only way was down when Gary Speed joined Bolton Wanderers for the next stage of his career. In fact nothing could have been further from the truth. As Newcastle nosedived and were eventually relegated in subsequent seasons to the Championship, Speed became part of a Bolton boom era which saw the Lancashire club celebrate their best days for almost a century.

As one of the Football League's founder clubs when they were formed back in 1888, Bolton had enjoyed a rich heritage but that was very much deep into yesteryear. Three times in the 1920s, in 1923, 1926 and 1929, they had won the FA Cup at Wembley. Bolton once again lifted the trophy in 1958 when two goals from Nat Lofthouse, their most famous son, accounted for Manchester United in another Wembley final. Since then, they had fallen on harder times, becoming something of a yo-yo club as they flitted up and down between the various four main divisions of English football.

Speed's arrival coincided with a dramatic change in fortunes. A revolution at the Reebok Stadium, which had begun when Sam Allardyce became manager in 1999, really gathered momentum when Speed put pen to paper on a £750,000 transfer from Newcastle in the summer of 2004. Speed was in his 35th year when he signed, an age when most footballers have retired, are thinking about hanging up their boots or, at the very best, find themselves slowing down quite demonstrably. He, however, proved to be as good as ever.

The secret of Bolton's success was Allardyce's bold strategy to fill his team with "been there, seen it, done it" veterans of world football, believing that together they could defy their combined age and instead use their experience to bring unprecedented success to the Reebok. Allardyce had already shown himself to be a skilled recruiter of ageing yet highly talented footballers. In previous seasons he had signed 36-year-old Youri Djorkaeff, who had been a key figure in helping France win the World Cup and the European Championships of 1998 and 2000 respectively. Although he was to leave in the close season before Speed arrived, Allardyce repeated similar signing successes. As a result, Speed shared the Bolton dressing room with the Nigerian playmaker Jay-Jay Okocha, another who shone in the 1998 World Cup, and former Real Madrid veteran central defender Ivan Campo was also on board, as was 87-times-capped legendary former Spanish captain Fernando Hierro.

Two more highly experienced players, ex-England striker Les Ferdinand and Senegal's El-Hadji Diouf, as well as French forward Nicolas Anelka, were further recruits in Allardyce's League of all Nations. Central to this, though, was the acquisition of Gary Speed, whom Allardyce had fought hard to sign, knowing there was competition from Middlesbrough, Fulham, Wolves and Speed's first club, Leeds United.

Speed offered Leeds the courtesy of talking to them, the least he could do given the happy eight years spent at Elland Road at the beginning of his career. However, once he had spoken to Allardyce, his heart and mind were set on Bolton. He explained: "I did well for Newcastle, played every game for them last season, and I wasn't expecting to leave, but I really believe I can take things on now for Bolton. There is so much more to be done still and I'm feeling as fit as ever. I am starting a new and, I hope, potentially exciting phase in my career." He even joked: "I was the oldest player at Newcastle and it's quite nice to lose that tag what with one or two of the others here at Bolton!"

On a more serious note, he pointed out: "People will go on about how old everyone is, but the fitness regime at Bolton is such that if you are not fit enough to play in the Premiership then you won't, whether you are 21, 31 or 41. I don't think age comes into it too much; what we have are some very good, very experienced players. You are never too old to learn. Sam has already opened my eyes with the way the club is run, so hopefully I can improve again."

Speed was referring to Allardyce's painstaking preparation for matches. The forward-thinking Bolton boss had armed himself with a 24-man backroom staff of sports science experts, individuals specifically identified and handpicked to help keep the legs and brains of the oldies the club had recruited performing at optimum level. Of course Speed himself had been given an early introduction to this side of top-level sport under Howard Wilkinson at Leeds, but Allardyce took it onto a whole new level with video analysis of his own players as well as the opposition team, sports psychology, nutritionists, masseurs and weekly blood, urine and saliva tests. This high-tech approach had a huge impact on Speed as a player in prolonging his career and then later as a manager and coach.

Allardyce was also a firm believer in cryotherapy, the below-freezing ice bath treatment designed to aid blood flow to the muscles and speed up the injury-healing process for sportsmen. Then a revolutionary practice, it evidently worked because Speed was able to play 45 high-profile matches during that first season with Bolton, including every single one of the club's 38 Premier League ties. The first of those, his debut game, was a 4-1 thumping of Charlton on August 14, 2004, which saw Bolton go straight to the top of the table. They would win three of their opening four matches, also defeating Liverpool and Southampton, and lost only one of their first seven fixtures away to Fulham.

Allardyce's backroom staff included computer analysts, who took a close look at data surrounding the Bolton players during matches and in training, including how much they ran, how quickly and their overall work-rate and therefore contribution to the cause. They would then give the figures to the manager, who used them to determine team selection. That sort of information, when fed into computers, could also have a bearing on who was substituted in matches.

The first reaction of the Bolton boss, on learning of Speed's own figures, was one of shock: "His statistics were off the map, awesome. He has a huge amount of energy and I imagine he possesses a bigger lung capacity than any normal human being. For somebody aged 34 to be able to run like a 24-year-old is pretty huge.

Reflecting on that golden period for the club, Allardyce recalls: "I guess I was very fortunate to take Gary to Bolton. He was available and willing to come to us for what I thought was a bargain price. In age terms, he was 34 and one or two questioned the fee at the time, but in every other sense his value to us was absolutely priceless. Okay, there would be no financial return in terms of selling him on in the future, but you couldn't put a price upon what he gave us in terms of experience, quality of football, leadership and know-how.

The fact that he was never injured and always wanted to play made him one of the most outstanding signings I ever made. I wanted to rest Gary in the odd match but if I suggested that he quickly told me, 'Forget it, I'd like to play.'

"It's difficult enough for players in their twenties to stay fit, let alone someone well into his thirties, as Gary was, but he had had a great year for club and country before joining us, including playing in big Wales games plus UEFA Champions League matches for Newcastle, and it was a no-brainer for me that he would do a fantastic job for Bolton Wanderers. We got exactly what we thought we would with Gary: someone who was greatly talented, dedicated, committed and who connected really well with his fellow players.

"We spent lots of time talking about the sports science side of things and no club had the level of support back-up that we did in those days. When we first showed it all to Gary, he was somewhat wide-mouthed – like all players are, in fact. As with other experienced players, Gary reckoned he had learned by then how his body worked, what was best for it, what wasn't, but once the fully qualified sports science staff we employed presented the information and data to Gary, he quickly came on board and realized it could help him continue to play to maximum performance for a number of extra years.

"This sort of sports science support back-up is commonplace these days at football clubs, of course, but back then there were some people who laughed at us. 'Why do you keep 24 members of staff for this sort of thing?' they would ask, but those employees had been chosen by me over a period of time because I could see their value to the players. With Gary, and everyone else at the club, it quickly became part of the day-to-day life of a Bolton Wanderers footballer. Once the players already on our books were convinced, they convinced the new players who came in. Thus it was the norm for us."

Two months into the season, with Bolton still riding high, Speed was to make an enormous decision that would further extend his club career. In October 2004, he travelled to Cardiff for two must-win Wales World Cup qualifying matches: against England at Old Trafford and then Poland at the Millennium Stadium. Mark Hughes's Wales side lost the two games and by the time Speed drove back to the North-west for Bolton's next Premier League match, a 1-0 home win over Crystal Palace on October 16, he was a former international footballer.

Wales's qualifying campaign was not even halfway through by that point, but they had taken only two points out of a possible 12 from their opening four fixtures, disappointingly drawing earlier games against Azerbaijan and Northern Ireland. With the prospects for the team reaching the 2006 finals in Germany close to zero, Speed decided it was time to hang up his international boots.

It was a huge call, Speed becoming just one of a number of seasoned old Wales war-horses to retire from playing for their country after the 3-2 home defeat to Poland. Others never again to appear for Wales included defender Andrew Melville and midfielders Robbie Savage and Mark Pembridge. However, Speed was the one missing figure that John Toshack, brought in to replace Hughes following the Polish loss, really wishes he could have kept on board: "Gary's experience would have been invaluable in helping to guide through a crop of youngsters we had to introduce into the team," he said.

Speed's view was that resting during international date windows would enable him to shake off any little niggles, freshen him up for domestic football and thus extend his club career. In that he wasn't wrong and he continued to excel as Bolton embarked on a five-match winning streak, defeating Birmingham (2-1), Arsenal (1-0), Blackburn (1-0), Tottenham (3-1) and Crystal Palace (1-0) to remain in the hunt for a European spot. But first he had to contend with calls from some of his former Wales teammates, including the vociferous Robbie Savage, for him to become the new manager of Wales. At that stage, he had no experience of coaching, let alone managing a team, but neither had Hughes when the FA of Wales handed him the job in the autumn of 1999, nor indeed had Mike England, one of Sparky's predecessors in the Welsh hot-seat.

Speed discussed the matter with Allardyce but contended: "I don't think I could give the role my full attention. We want the best man for the job and I don't think that's me at the moment. I definitely won't be applying for it."

Deep down, Allardyce must have been pleased, knowing if Speed was 100 per cent focused on Bolton Wanderers, they would be the beneficiaries. "All Gary wants to do is play as long as he can. When you give up international football, you have a better chance of a longer career," he said at the time. "That is what it is all about. Gary needs a contract; he needs to be paid by a club and play at the highest level he possibly can for as long as he can. The international side of it doesn't come into play because they don't have a contract with him, so that is the first thing you should give up.

"He needs a rest sometimes, but he just doesn't want one with Bolton. I have had a massive problem leaving him out of our FA Cup games. He has been moaning and groaning at me because he has even wanted to play in those matches."

There was never any question of Speed being rested for any of Bolton's Premier League matches as they pushed hard for Europe and on April 30, 2005, he took part in another of the landmark matches that featured throughout his career. The game in question, against

Chelsea at the Reebok Stadium, went down in footballing history as the day when the London team won their first League title for 50 years: two second-half goals from Frank Lampard ensured the Premier trophy was theirs and the charismatic José Mourinho had begun his managerial stint in British football with a major honour.

Understandably, the exploits of Lampard, Mourinho and Chelsea's talismanic captain, John Terry, captured the headlines. The game was also significant, though, as the 700th club match of Speed's career – a quite extraordinary feat. He tested Chelsea goalkeeper Petr Cech with a header which forced a good save, but was content to stay out of the limelight that afternoon, although he did play well in Bolton's remaining League games away to Portsmouth (1-1) the following week and at home to Everton (3-2 win) seven days on again to help the Trotters seal sixth spot in the table. It may have been Chelsea's first title since 1955, but it was also Bolton's best-ever finish in the Premier League and ensured that they would be able to compete in the prestigious UEFA Cup in the following 2005–06 season.

For the record, Newcastle – the club Speed had left behind – finished in a lowly 14th place and looked warily over their shoulders towards the bottom of the table rather than pushing for further European adventures.

Speed was loving his time under Allardyce and particularly relished the way the sports science approach was extending his career at the top level: "The good thing from a personal point of view is that they look after me well. It is a very professionally run club and they get the best out of the players. For someone my age, with the amount of games I've played, it's fantastic, because every time I step on the pitch, I feel as fresh as a daisy."

Which is why he featured in another 40 matches the following season, including a march to the third round of the UEFA Cup, the first time Bolton had appeared in that competition before the dream was ended with a 2-1 defeat to French giants Marseille in February 2006. In the Premier League Bolton finished eighth, another highly commendable effort, and their results included a thumping 4-0 victory over Everton at Goodison Park just before Christmas in 2005. Speed, who scored one of his side's goals that day, must have experienced something of a bittersweet emotion, given that Everton were the team he grew up supporting as a boy. However, he knew his priority at this point was Bolton and was once more at his exemplary best in the 2006–07 campaign, yet again featuring in every single one of Bolton's 38 Premier League matches, even though he was well into his 38th year by the time another highly successful season was over.

That year, as Bolton finished seventh to once more qualify for Europe, Speed had his best goal return for the club, scoring eight times, and inevitably there were some crucial ones among them. Like the winning goals against Aston Villa, Fulham and Watford and another excellent strike during a 2-0 triumph over Liverpool, a result which sent Bolton second in the Premier League table.

It was during that particular season that another Speed landmark was reached. On December 9, 2006, he became the first player to make 500 Premier League appearances when helping Bolton to batter West Ham 4-0 in front of 22,283 fans at the Reebok. Kevin Davies (2), Nicolas Anelka and El-Hadji Diouf scored the goals that day, but Speed, perhaps predictably given his knack of rising to the occasion, was named official Man of the Match. Newspaper reports the following day stated he had "bossed the midfield and outplayed younger and supposedly fitter opponents". Incidentally, those opponents included Argentine superstar Carlos Tevez and England goalkeeper Robert Green. Even the great Tevez was no match for

Speed that afternoon and Hammers manager Alan Pardew would lose his job as a result of his side's 4-0 loss.

The tributes poured in for Speed, led by Gordon Taylor, chairman of the players' union, the Professional Footballers Association. "For Gary to feature in so many matches is a tribute to his fitness and skill levels," purred Taylor. "When you look at the job he has done for various clubs, and for his country, you can see he is one of our finest members. You have to admire him for his exemplary record."

Bolton's skipper that afternoon, Kevin Nolan, stated admiringly: "He just goes on and on, and season by season seems to get younger and fitter – and faster. Gary is 37 going on 38, but he's still like a 21-year-old. I just can't see any sign of him stopping yet, either."

As for Speed himself, he gave a typical response when quizzed by the media about his record-breaking achievement after the West Ham game. "What mattered most was not Gary Speed making his 500th Premiership appearance, but Bolton getting a much-needed three points," he said in customary modest fashion. "We had been on a bad run and dipped down the table a bit and had to come out of that. It was a much-needed three points and hopefully that means the end to our bad spell. I enjoyed a glass of wine afterwards but if we hadn't won, I would have been sitting in sulking on Saturday night.

"I will look back on landmarks when I retire and obviously I will have pride then, but I don't pay a lot of attention to them at the moment. It makes me feel old, for starters, whenever people mention this record! I'm just out to keep playing, don't count how many games I rack up. It's not that these records don't mean anything to me, it's just that it's a team game and we are a close-knit team at Bolton; it's not about individuals. I will hang my boots up one day and that will be the time to look back on what I've achieved, but not at the moment."

As a result of their victory over the Hammers, Bolton moved up to fifth in the table, a position they were to retain right up until six matches before the end of the season, when Speed once more played a starring role as they defeated Wigan 3-1 away from home.

With those final half-dozen games to go, Allardyce believed that his team could do even better by pushing for a top-four spot and thus grab a dream place in the UEFA Champions League the following season. Little Bolton, tangling with Europe's elite crack sides such as Barcelona, Real Madrid, AC Milan and Bayern Munich – it was a mouth-watering prospect. However, the vision disappeared as Bolton failed to win any of those final six games, losing to Arsenal, Reading and West Ham and drawing with Everton, Chelsea and Aston Villa. They finished seventh, still an excellent achievement, because it once more secured them a place in the following season's UEFA Cup competition. But for Allardyce it wasn't enough. Out of the blue he shocked everyone, Speed included, by quitting at the end of April 2007, just two games before the end of the season. Rightly or wrongly, he felt that he needed more support to make that last push towards the top.

Explaining his decision, Allardyce says: "Bolton, at the end, had an opportunity to finish in the Champions League but didn't seem to want to take it, so what was the point in staying? As much as I loved the club, it was impossible for me to stay. We had 39 points after 21 games. We were ahead of Arsenal, ahead of Liverpool. We needed to spend some money to bring in new players. All we had to do was have a mediocre 17 games and we were going to finish in the Champions League. The players were too fatigued to carry on because we had a smaller squad than Manchester United, Arsenal, Liverpool and Chelsea."

Allardyce says the new signings did not materialize, so he walked away. His departure saddened Speed, but, as the saying goes, when one door closes, another one opens. In this case he was handed the opportunity to become player-coach, as part of the backroom team under new manager Sammy Lee. On taking up his new appointment, Speed said: "Big Sam has created a legacy that everyone is proud of here at Bolton, but everyone knows that football must go on and we have the responsibility of taking Bolton forward."

One of Lee's first moves on landing the manager's job was to appoint Speed in his coaching role, saying at the time: "Gary is a model professional and has great aspirations to be a top-class coach. He is a highly qualified, having recently gained his UEFA A licence. He has great tactical and technical knowledge and is highly respected by his teammates."

At the time, Speed seemed enthusiastic enough about the immediate future but in actual fact things were never again so good at Bolton and his flirtation with the coaching side turned out to be all too brief. After just eight fixtures of the following season's 2007–08 Premier League campaign, he was back to being a plain old player again.

Bolton won just one of those opening eight league matches and languished in 19th position, only able to remain off the very bottom because of goal difference. This run of poor results meant that changes needed to be made and it was announced that Speed would no longer be the Bolton coach, following a 1-0 home loss to Chelsea on October 7, 2007. So, did he go of his own accord or was he pushed? There were conflicting reports at the time. Lee said: "I relieved Gary of his coaching duties because I want him to focus on his game – I don't want anything to distract him from that." In response, Speed stated: "It was my decision, I decided it wasn't working out. I want to concentrate totally on my football."

These differing versions of events came against a backdrop of newspaper reports in which it was speculated that some of the senior players were not overly enamoured by Lee's management style. It was claimed that Speed had grown increasingly frustrated with Lee for ignoring his advice about how the ailing team should play. Speed, as well as club captain Kevin Nolan, was left out of that defeat to Chelsea and just days afterwards Lee was himself relieved of his management duties. Ricky Sbragia, another member of Allardyce's old backroom coaching team, took charge of the next match, a 2-0 defeat against Arsenal on October 20, 2007, before Gary Megson became Speed's third full-time Bolton manager in the space of just six months. What had been such an amazing journey for his first three seasons at the club had now turned into something of a nightmare for Speed.

Under Megson's watch, Speed was at least straight back into the starting XI, with a 1-1 draw with Aston Villa next up on October 25, 2007. Deep down, he knew this was the beginning of the end of his extraordinary run in top-flight football, though. He featured just six times more for Bolton, one of those matches being a memorable 1-0 home win over Sir Alex Ferguson's Manchester United on November 24, 2007, which lifted the Trotters up to 15th position in the table. However, three matches in the space of six days at the beginning of December proved to be Speed's Bolton swansong. The first of those, played on December 2, 2007, was his last start as a Premier League footballer. He played for the full 90 minutes that day against Liverpool at Anfield as two goals from Steven Gerrard, another from Fernando Torres and a Ryan Babel strike gave the Reds a 4-0 victory.

"It was a poor day and we'll pick ourselves up. There won't be any knee-jerk reaction to this," was Megson's pragmatic after-match assessment. Knee-jerk or not, he would barely use Speed again following the Anfield annihilation. Speed did play the following week when Bolton travelled abroad to beat Red Star Belgrade 1-0 in the UEFA Cup, a Gavin McCann goal handing them victory. Speed, one of only a handful of Bolton players to retain his place in the team following the Liverpool loss, was made captain for the night.

It proved to be a fitting send-off for such a great servant, because three days on, when Bolton were back home to host Wigan in their next Premier League game, Speed was sent on only as a 90th-minute substitute for Ivan Campo in a 4-1 victory for the Trotters on December 9, 2007. He barely had time to even touch the ball, but after almost 18 years at that level, dating back to the sunny August day in 1990 when he played for Leeds against Wimbledon in the old First Division, it was to be the last time that he would walk onto the pitch as a top-flight footballer.

Bolton played four more matches that December, losing to Manchester City, Everton and Sunderland and beating Birmingham, but Speed was not to feature in any of those fixtures under Megson. By the time Bolton played again in the New Year, achieving a 1-0 win over Derby County at the Reebok, Speed had departed for pastures new with Sheffield United in the Championship. "I'm not in the team at Bolton. I've no complaints about that – the team are playing well, but I need to be playing games," said Speed. "I am fit enough to play. I have not got much time left and I want to play football."

That season Bolton would finish 16th, a real low after the record-breaking highs of Speed's first three years with the club. According to Allardyce, though, the disappointing ending should not detract from Speed's hugely successful time in the North-west. "He was a great pleasure to work with and together we enjoyed big success with the club," says Allardyce. "We didn't win the Premier

League title but we broke new ground for Bolton Wanderers, achieved things the club had never previously managed in their entire history. Bolton Wanderers were 100 years old, but had never played European football before. We qualified for the UEFA Cup two times out of three seasons.

"Gary was a key part of everything we did, made a major contribution to our team. We came very, very close towards the end of my reign (Gary's third year) to getting that Champions League spot, which for a club of Bolton's size would have been an unbelievable achievement. Gary offered more than just football ability, though. You should look beyond the footballer on the field of play and think also of the man. As a man, he was just as special as he was as a footballer.

"Like most players he would like a good old moan now and again, but he was always willing to help others and they all looked up to him. Gary was the consummate professional. When younger players would slip in standards, I would say to them: 'Just take a look at Speedo. If he can do it at his age, then why can't you do it?' In that respect, he was a perfect tool for me to put up there as a figurehead role model they could all follow.

"Gary was an all-time great of the game and the only thing that has stopped him having an even greater profile was the fact that Wales haven't been to a European Championship or a World Cup. Had they done that, he and Ryan Giggs would be held in even greater esteem throughout the world game. Players like Robbie Keane and Damien Duff are held in high regard because they have played at World Cup level for the Republic of Ireland. Unfortunately, Gary and Ryan never had that luxury. Make no mistake, though, Gary was a top, top player, who in my view also possessed the qualities to become a top coach and then a top manager."

Those words might be said in hindsight, but Allardyce also believed them at the time, for he urged Speed to go out and get his coaching qualifications. Given what was to happen in subsequent years, Allardyce's advice would prove wonderfully prophetic.

9

The End …
and a New Beginning

"I wouldn't forgive myself if I hadn't given it a shot."
Gary Speed – on taking his first football management job

After 18 years and well in excess of 800 matches played at the highest level, an achievement matched only by fellow Welsh great Ryan Giggs in modern times, Gary Speed stepped back down to where it all began for the final chapter of his playing career.

On New Year's Day of 2008, Speed signed and that afternoon made his debut for Sheffield United, snapped up by then Blades manager Bryan Robson, the England and Manchester United legend, who saw him as the wise old head who could guide Sheffield United back into the big time. The Yorkshire outfit had just been relegated after one brief season in the Premier League and stood a lowly 16th in the Championship when Speed came on board; they were hoping his experience and footballing know-how could help spark a surge up the table into the promotion positions.

When Speed made his debut on that cold January 1 day, a dreary 0-0 draw away to Wolverhampton Wanderers at Molineux, it was his first game of football outside the top flight since a Bank Holiday Monday in May 1990, when he helped Leeds United clinch the old Second Division title with a 1-0 win against Harry Redknapp's Bournemouth. In the year that he joined Sheffield United, Speed's influence would help them climb as high as eighth position in the table, but they were never in serious consideration for promotion.

That debut match with his new club, however, signified the both beginning of the end for Speed's playing days and also the dawn of a new era. Later that year, he would play the final match of a glittering career that had lasted 20 years, stretching back to his debut for Leeds at home to Oldham, back in 1988. But Sheffield United also handed Speed a number of opportunities, including the chance to take his first steps into full-time coaching.

Accepting that his 38-year-old legs had probably seen their best days at Premier League level, Speed still hankered after playing at as high a standard as possible and believed a go-ahead club like Sheffield United, who were in the next division down, presented an ideal opportunity. Robson had chased his man for some time, admitting: "I tried to get Gary before the season started but Bolton wouldn't release him. I spoke to them again, got the same answer, so it has been an ongoing thing until I succeeded. Gary was in a very successful side at Bolton and I am pleased to get him. He is a very experienced player, a 'youthful' late-thirties type of footballer, whose knowledge will be invaluable to us."

Speed or no Speed, sadly for Robson his Blades were about to embark on a winless run and he was quickly replaced in the manager's hot-seat by Kevin Blackwell. Speed had only been with his new club for a matter of weeks when the man who had pursued him so hotly to clinch his signature departed. Even approaching his 40th birthday, though, Speed was such a good player that any incoming manager would have been a fool not to build his team around the Welsh veteran. Kevin Blackwell, the candidate selected to replace Robson, immediately saw Speed's value, asked him to pull the strings for the team and at least Sheffield United were able to complete a pretty strong ending to the season.

They won eight of their last 11 matches to get some sort of momentum going into the 2008–09 campaign, which would prove to be Speed's last as a professional player. The season started brightly enough, with Sheffield United winning nine and drawing four out of their first 18 League matches, putting them in fourth position in the table and establishing themselves as credible contenders for a push for automatic promotion to the Premier League. Speed played in 17 of those games, as well as a Carling Cup defeat to Arsenal at the Emirates, and was his customary consistent, excellent and unflappable self. But just as he began his Blades spell with a game against Wolves, so he was suddenly to finish against them as a player as well, the final curtain coming down on his playing career on a Tuesday evening in November 2008 when 27,111 flocked to Bramall Lane to witness an unfortunate 3-1 defeat for Blackwell's team.

There had been no sign whatsoever of any problems to come for Speed when, in the previous match, he had scored yet another goal in his career to help Sheffield United thump Charlton 5-2. The Blades were displaying a cutting edge and in the dressing room the quiet talk was of promotion that season, whether automatically or via the play-offs. However, just 10 minutes of the game against Wolves had elapsed when Speed suddenly felt a twinge in his back, making it hard for him even to move. He wasn't the type to come off unless he really had to, but on this occasion he had no option but to limp out of the action. It was to be the last time anyone saw Gary Speed on the field of play.

Blackwell sent on Matthew Spring, a relative unknown. A midfielder who had played for Leyton Orient, Charlton, Luton and Watford in the lower divisions, Spring was something of a journeyman footballer. He provided the one moment of joy on the night when he scored Sheffield's solitary goal, 15 minutes from time.

As the days wore on, Speed noticed shooting pains down the right-hand side of his leg, mixed with occasional numbness. This was clearly not just an ordinary type of football injury, which generally means one or two weeks out before the player is back in the thick of the action. The Sheffield United medics advised a hospital scan and the results quickly determined that Speed had a protruded disc in his back that was touching on the nerves and causing the pain. It was advised that he underwent surgery, but the player himself remained upbeat, saying: "I can't wait for the operation and to start getting back to fitness again."

No one, least of all Speed himself, believed this to be a long-term problem. Unable to play for the time being, he took his first tentative steps into coaching on a voluntary basis and offered vocal encouragement from the sidelines as Sheffield United finished third in the League, denied automatic promotion by Wolves and Birmingham before being agonizingly beaten 1-0 by Burnley in the play-off final at Wembley in May 2009.

At first Speed had anticipated playing a full part in that promotion run-in at the business end of the season – the time of year when, as we have seen from his spell as a Leeds player, he tended to shine in the high-pressure matches that really mattered. Asked shortly after surgery whether his playing days could be over, he declared: "No, I'm not finished yet. I've spoken to the surgeon involved in quite some detail and although March or April of next year could be too soon to come back, I do think that I can return before the end of the season and have some part to play. I want to finish the season with Sheffield United and then we will go from there, but I think I can make the last month or so, when it could be an interesting time for the club. The surgeon said that this kind of disc trouble is most common between the ages of 38 and 42, but I know a lot of players who have had similar injuries at 26 or 27, so I guess I have been very lucky on the injury front for almost my entire career."

It was typical of him to put a positive slant on such worrying times. Behind the scenes, he received intensive treatment and worked as hard as he could, considering his lack of mobility, to try and get his fitness back and return to the playing fold. For someone who hadn't had a serious injury and had played almost constantly for two decades, it was an incredibly frustrating period, but as the days and weeks passed and then turned into months, Speed privately began to accept that this was the end of his playing career. Although pain-free and able to run, he admitted: "The nerve is hindering some of the muscles in my leg so I don't have the speed or power I need to play football. I wish I was playing, but I can't at the moment."

Giving the appearance of having accepted his fate, just after the start of the 2009–10 campaign Speed went public by saying: "I've had a great career and if this is the moment I stop playing then we will have to see what opportunities come my way and decide from there. What I also have to consider is whether I can afford to continue playing football if it has a physical effect on me for future years. I'm 40, haven't played for a year. I'm not missing playing, I'm enjoying the other side of football."

That "other side of football" he mentioned was his break into coaching after Sheffield United's go-ahead chairman Kevin McCabe spotted real potential in him for such a role. The sort of leadership skills, one presumes, that Howard Wilkinson first picked up on many years ago at Leeds when, with Speed just 22 years of age, he had the foresight to call him into his office and tell him he was destined to one day become a manager. Speed had had a brief flirtation with coaching while at Bolton but the first real step towards that career pathway came when he joined Blackwell's backroom team on a permanent basis. Day in, day out, he worked as a hands-on coach next to the vastly experienced Sam Ellis, who had done the rounds as manager of Blackpool, Bury and Lincoln, and who had also been round the block as a lower-division player with Mansfield, Lincoln City and Watford.

Explaining the decision, McCabe says: "Having seen Gary as a player for many years, it just seemed to me he was a fine example of a true professional footballer who was rarely over the top in anything he did or said. His conduct as a hard-working player actually got better as he got older. In that respect, he was very similar to Bryan Robson, an example others could follow. What Gary did was bound to rub off on the rest of the players.

"When Robbo, as manager, first brought Gary to us for what was going to be the last move of his career, the plan was always to bring him in as a player-coach. Robbo definitely believed Gary had the credentials to become a top-class manager in due course. That was in our minds at the time of the signing. Whether Gary would actually be manager of Sheffield United as part of a succession plan, or whether working with us would help him get a manager's job elsewhere, you could just logically see management coming so naturally for Gary.

"He put the coaching plans on hold to begin with by playing for a season and a bit, but age then got the better of him. He picked up the back injury, was in too much discomfort to play on any more and transferred from being a player-coach with us to more of a coach-player. At that stage Robbo was gone, of course, and Gary was learning the new side of the trade next to Kevin Blackwell and Sam Ellis. The technical part was easy for Gary because of what he had done over the course of so many years as a player and captain. That he could get the best out of those around him was already evident, but there were off-field things – coaching drills and the like – that he could learn from Sam. Here he was learning that side of the job from someone who had been there, seen it; done it. Even at that stage I told him that if anything happened, we would like him to one day take over the reins at Bramall Lane. I knew we had a very good young manager in the making here, someone with fresh ideas. Within 15 months of Gary Speed being at Sheffield United, the seeds were planted in my mind of the possibility of him becoming our manager one day."

Those seeds continued to grow during the 2009–10 season when, according to McCabe, Sheffield United punched below their weight. He had expected the Blades to earn promotion under Blackwell. Instead they finished a disappointing eighth, five points behind Ian Holloway's Blackpool, who sneaked into the last play-off spot and went on to reach Premier League dreamland by defeating Cardiff City 3-2 at Wembley in May 2010. Newcastle United and West Bromwich Albion took the two automatic promotion spots.

"Towards the latter part of that season we were dreadful at times, to be honest," is McCabe's no-holds-barred assessment of what went wrong. "We lost our strategy, in my view, relied upon too many loan players. The odd one such as Leon Britton, whom we had signed on a permanent deal from Swansea, was good but others were simply not up to it. The style of football we played, though, didn't suit Leon, a midfield player who liked to pass the ball around – something he does extremely well, as he has subsequently proved with Swansea City in the Premier League. Leon couldn't get a kick with us because the ball was four feet airborne above his head too often!"

So commenced the 2010–11 season and an extraordinary five-month period which saw Speed almost achieve a bizarre playing comeback, among other developments. Somewhere in between there was also an approach from Swansea City, who wanted to talk to him about their managerial vacancy following the departure of former Portugal and Juventus star Paulo Sousa, whose time in charge of the Welsh club had come to an end. Sheffield United, however, said they refused permission for Speed to leave and so Swansea had to look elsewhere. Not that it did them much harm: the Swansea board of directors instead approached Brendan Rodgers, a member of the Chelsea coaching team, and he took them up into the Premier League.

For Speed, the whirlwind period at Bramall Lane began in ignominious fashion as Sheffield United, still with Blackwell at the helm, drew their first match of the season at Cardiff, were thumped 3-0 at home by Neil Warnock's Queens Park Rangers in their next league encounter and suffered the humiliation of a 2-0 Carling Cup defeat at lower-division Hartlepool United. A recorded crowd of precisely 2,520 witnessed that drab Cup affair on a Wednesday night, August 11, 2010, the match being settled by goals from Hartlepool's James Brown after six minutes and Adam Boyd in the second half. For Blackwell, it was embarrassing. His team were unable to muster a single shot on target until substitute Kyle Bartley (sent on in the 82nd minute) tested the Hartlepool goalkeeper at the end of the match.

Sitting next to Bartley that night in his kit was Speed. Though he had by then formally announced his retirement, he had been registered as a player and ready to come on, should Blackwell decree. Thankfully he wasn't asked to do so – it would have been an entirely unfitting way for him to bow out.

Four days on, with Sheffield United suffering more misery as they were hammered at home by QPR, the writing was well and truly on the wall for Blackwell. With the season just three matches old, he was duly sacked and Speed promoted to the manager's post. Blackwell's number two, Sam Ellis, was also dismissed as part of the shake-up and, at first, Speed believed he himself was also on the way out. Instead, McCabe (who lives in Brussels and works as a businessman abroad) asked him to travel out by train to meet him in Belgium and discuss becoming the main man. Speed promptly caught the Eurostar and, folllowing a constructive meeting with the Blades chairman, terms and conditions were quickly agreed and the decision was announced on August 17, 2010.

McCabe says: "Blackwell got his formations wrong and a change had to be made. Within 24 to 48 hours of making that decision, I had brought Gary on board as manager. That hunch I had first had a year or so earlier came to fruition, I guess. I arranged for Gary to travel out on Eurostar to Brussels to meet me to discuss the job and I recall to this day how I had to hurriedly make a journey to Lille instead because heavy rain and flash flooding meant the Eurostar service couldn't go as far as normal and had to terminate at Lille.

"Pretty much the first thing Gary told me was that he wanted Sam Ellis brought back as his assistant. That shocked me, to be honest. Why? Because he had already made a decision: coaches adhere to decisions, managers make them and he was making one already even though the job hadn't formally been agreed yet. He wanted the man who had just departed from the club at his side, so Sam Ellis was reinstated within 24 hours of being told he wasn't required any more! But good on Gary, he knew his own mind and I was more confident than ever, by that stage, that he would make a terrific manager for Sheffield United."

In time, the McCabes became very close to Speed and his family. Kevin's son, Simon, and his wife, Katey, spent time away with the Speeds – Gary, his wife, Louise, and their two sons, Ed and Thomas – at a holiday home they owned in the south of France. Simon McCabe also ran the New York marathon with Louise, who was a keen runner.

Among the McCabes there was a real optimism that Speed would quickly develop into a top young manager, one of the new modern-day breed, if you like, although things didn't quite start off as planned.

Speed's first match as a manager was on August 22, 2010, when he took his team for a Championship tie away to Middlesbrough at the Riverside. That day Sheffield United turned in a much improved performance but Kris Boyd scored the only goal of the game for Boro after 52 minutes and with the other teams near the foot of the table achieving wins or draws, Speed's side suddenly found themselves rock bottom of the table. Of course after that the only way could be up and McCabe was in no doubt whatsoever that the Blades would soon hit their stride under Speed's guidance.

"I was of the belief that Gary had inherited a team which required restructuring and he needed time to put his mark upon things," explains McCabe. "Morale wasn't great because we were not winning. We had lost Chris Morgan, our captain and perhaps the best centre-back in the Championship, to a knee cruciate ligament injury. Darius Henderson, perhaps the best centre-forward in the Championship, was also out with a cruciate ligament problem. Our goalkeeper, Paddy Kenny, left to join Queens Park Rangers. However, despite these issues I was fully confident about Gary turning things around, even more so when I started to get to know him better. I used to see him regularly on a Saturday morning before games, when we talked about life in general, not just football, as a way of him getting settled before kick-off. He was more of an old-fashioned type of professional footballer in terms of his ideals – there was nothing wishy-washy about Gary – and I was convinced that sort of honesty and approach would pay off in time with our players."

Speed himself at first feared the bullet when Blackwell was dismissed following the loss to Queens Park Rangers. He believed

McCabe would bring in an outsider, someone who would want his own coaching team around him. "On the Saturday night after the QPR match I thought I was out of a job, so I didn't know anything about this. Myself, Kevin Blackwell and Sam Ellis had a great open relationship in that respect," he told the local newspaper the Sheffield *Star* at the time. "When the club had earlier refused permission for me to speak to Swansea, I phoned Kevin straight away because I didn't want a hidden agenda there and he was 100 per cent behind me and very understanding.

"Ideally I would have spent more time preparing myself for management under Kevin but football is about opportunities. I have had a couple of management chances before and I didn't take them, but once it comes around at a club like this, I don't think it would come calling again if I said no. I am grateful and honoured to be in charge of a club with such great history and tradition; I would be a fool not to accept.

"The reason I want to be a manager is I wouldn't forgive myself if I hadn't given it a shot. I spoke to my wife briefly, but it wasn't really a discussion – she knew I was going to do it, so that was that, really. So she is going to be a long-suffering football manager's wife now, but she will support me. I could have gone into the media side of football but it is difficult to get back in if you don't take the opportunity when it presents itself. It will be hard work, but I have always been prepared to put the graft in. You can't change the style of play straight away, but I have firm ideas about how I want the team to play. I like passing football but it has also got to be winning football – we can't just pass and look nice."

Speed set about putting his words into action in the next game as Sheffield United defeated Preston 1-0 in front of a 19,682 crowd at Bramall Lane on August 28, 2010. It was his first home match in charge and he received a huge ovation from Blades fans when he walked out of the tunnel prior to kick-off after his team.

Speed's management vision was displayed as early as that very first match for he gave a debut that afternoon to a French defender called Jean Calvé, who responded by scoring the only goal of the game with a humdinger of a shot from fully 30 yards out. Ironically, Calvé immediately dropped to the turf with cramp in his legs and had to be instantly substituted. As he hobbled off, he gave Speed a warm embrace. Sheffield United were up and running with their first win of the season, climbing eight places off the bottom up to 17th in the table.

After that it was up and down for Speed. Over the course of the next three months his team achieved fine wins over Derby, Portsmouth, Hull, Millwall and Crystal Palace, drew with Burnley, Nottingham Forest and Leicester, but lost to Scunthorpe, Leeds, Watford, Doncaster, Coventry, Ipswich, Bristol City and Barnsley. The match with Barnsley – a 1-0 defeat at Oakwell played on December 11, 2010 – was settled by a first-half goal from Hugo Colace and pushed Sheffield United down to 20th in the table. By that stage the Blades had played 18 matches under Speed, won six, drawn three and lost nine. Their goals-scored tally read 15 and they had conceded 24 goals. It was a significant improvement on their earlier record at the start of the season but Sheffield United's lowly position in the table led to a few murmurings about whether the team was in real danger of going down under Speed. That disquiet was quickly overtaken by speculation that Wales were ready to swoop for their former captain, asking him to become full-time manager. The talk had come somewhat out of the blue because Speed did not even feature upon an earlier six-man Football Association of Wales shortlist. However, as the hours passed, it became clear that he was the man that Wales really wanted. By the time Sheffield United played next, ironically against Swansea City on December 18, the Welsh club who were themselves reported to have been keen on Speed as manager just a few months earlier, he had left to take charge of his country instead.

Blades managerial legend Dave "Harry" Bassett, who won three promotions with Sheffield United and took the club up into the Premier League during his stint in charge (1988–95), expressed surprise at Speed's decision. "The international scene, in my opinion at least, is something that you look to get into 15 or 20 years down the line," he told the Sheffield *Star*. "Gary's a really nice lad and I respect him a lot, but surely if you are ambitious then you want to get a side like Sheffield United into the Premier League? I don't think the Wales job is bigger."

McCabe, who agreed a six-figure compensation deal with Wales to release Speed from his contract to allow them to bring him back home, begged to differ: "Gary was very proud – and quite rightly so – to be given the opportunity to lead his country. He left on very amicable terms. Some people were pointing to our lowly position in the Championship table at the time, but I honestly think if Gary had remained with us rather than gone with Wales, he would have got us out of the predicament we were in. He would have been able to bolster our squad in the January transfer window for starters. Just the name of Gary Speed, his reputation and the type of football he wanted to play would have been sufficient to attract leading players to Sheffield United. Throw in the fact that he was bright, intelligent and excellent at dealing with people and it was a no-brainer that he would succeed with us."

After Speed left Bramall Lane, Sheffield United endured a horrific final five months to the season, eventually finishing in 23rd spot –

just one off the very bottom – and finding themselves relegated into League One. It was the first time in 22 years that they had dropped down into the third tier of English football. With Speed at the helm, McCabe is convinced this would never have happened and, if anything, Sheffield United would have gone in exactly the opposite direction. But the man he saw as a top young manager in the making was about to achieve great things with his country in what was to be his last football hurrah.

10

Reviving the Hopes of a Nation

"Since [Gary] came in as manager, we feel we're improving all the time. We want to achieve something special for Wales, and we feel we can do it."

Gareth Bale – Wales winger

The fates, it appears, always seem to conspire against the Wales football team. There is an old saying in the sport, used by managers, players, pundits and fans, about luck balancing itself out over a period of time. If you don't have the rub of the green for a while, the wheel of fortune will invariably turn your way at some point. Try telling this to Wales managers, players or supporters over the course of many, many years, though. Successive Welsh teams must have been wondering whether, for the best part of five decades, their players had crossed black cats, walked under ladders and cracked mirrors, all in one go.

Joe Jordan is still something of a persona non grata to Welsh fans after the infamous handball incident which led to Scotland, not Wales, qualifying for the 1978 World Cup in Argentina. Jordan's arm went up in the box while being challenged by Wales's central defender David Jones and the referee inexplicably awarded a penalty kick to the Scots. Don Masson duly converted, Kenny Dalglish added a second and it was tournament over for the Dragons. A few years on and another highly contentious penalty kick decision once more cost Wales against the Scots, this time in a win-or-bust showdown at Cardiff's Ninian Park in the race for Mexico 1986. Dave Phillips was adjudged to have handled when the ball was whacked straight at him from close range, Glasgow Rangers star Davie Cooper converted and Wales were once again controversially eliminated.

As a kid growing up, Gary Speed watched those matches, but he was directly involved in his country's next two moments of misfortune. First, Paul Bodin's missed penalty against Romania cost Wales a place in the 1994 World Cup Finals in the United States. A decade on, Speed's hopes of appearing in the European Championships in Portugal in 2004 disappeared when Russia knocked them out of the play-offs, the two-legged tie marred by controversy surrounding their midfielder Igor Titov, who was found guilty of taking a banned performance-enhancing substance. Wales appealed to UEFA, FIFA and the Court of Arbitration for Sport in Switzerland, but to no avail.

The team then embarked on some dark days before Speed came on board as manager and offered real hope of them reaching the 2014 World Cup in Brazil. Sadly, the tragic events of November 27, 2011 saw that bubble of huge optimism deflated once more. For one reason or another, getting the Dragons to a major international finals was becoming football's equivalent of mission impossible. For a nation that has produced genuine greats of the world game, including Ryan Giggs, Ian Rush, Mark Hughes and Neville Southall, backed up by Kevin Ratcliffe, Craig Bellamy and Speed himself, the ongoing Welsh failure in both the World Cup and European Championships mystified many, particularly when Northern Ireland, Scotland and the Republic of Ireland had each achieved the feat on more than one occasion, all with arguably far less talented groups of footballers.

However, the Football Association of Wales believed they had landed the man to end the qualifying jinx, dating back to the last time when Wales reached a major finals at the 1958 World Cup in Sweden, when they appointed the worldly-wise and seasoned old campaigner John Toshack as their manager in November 2004. If anyone was to deliver the dream surely it would be "Big John", who had entered the Welsh post with the best credentials of all. Twice manager of Real Madrid, the world's biggest club, he had secured the Spanish La Liga title with a record number of points and goals during his first stint at the Bernabéu and boasted a wealth of experience from his time managing Sporting Lisbon in Portugal, Catania in Italy, Beşiktaş of Turkey and one-time French giants St Etienne. As well as bossing Real Madrid, he also had spells in charge of Deportivo de La Coruña and Real Sociedad in Spain.

Toshack was probably the right man at the wrong time, having inherited a team of players such as Speed himself, who were into their thirties, with many of them about to retire, and who had not won a single competitive game for a full two years under Mark Hughes. It was the worst possible combination, decreed Toshack: an ageing team and a losing one. He was left with a painstakingly difficult task, choosing to throw in a plethora of Welsh teenagers and early-20-somethings, who were clearly not yet ready for international football, though in effect learning their trade in the harshest environment of all. Among them were players who were barely heard of at the time, such as Gareth Bale and Aaron Ramsey – not necessarily in their club's first teams though eventually they would become household names.

Toshack's own man-management style, which was perceived by some as old-fashioned and alienated certain senior players, didn't help matters, according to pundits. Yet despite undertaking the biggest rebuilding job ever in Welsh international football, he still departed from the post after six years at the helm with the best winning record of any Wales manager in history. Of the 54 matches during which he was in charge (from February 2005 to September 2010), Wales won 41 per cent of them, although Toshack's critics – of whom there were many – would argue all too often the games won were not the key qualifiers that really mattered. Nonetheless, his winning record still eclipsed those of Mike England and Terry Yorath, managers with the previous best tallies. England, the man who led Wales during the 1980s, had a 39 per cent winning record from his 56 internationals as manager. Yorath, who succeeded him in the Wales hot-seat and kept the job until was sacked in 1993, also won 39 per cent of his 41 matches.

Englishman Mike Smith, who enjoyed two separate stints in charge during the 1970s and 1990s, won 38 per cent of his 40 matches. Mark Hughes, commonly seen outside Wales as a big managerial success story, perhaps surprisingly had a win ratio of just 29 per cent of the 41 matches during which he was in charge of the team, from September 1999 through to Speed's last match as a player against Poland at the Millennium Stadium in October 2004. Bobby Gould, commonly seen inside and outside Wales as a failure in the role of manager, had an identical wining figure of 29 per cent from his 24 games in charge during the 1990s. Going back to yesteryear, Jimmy Murphy secured 25 per cent of his matches as manager, while Dave Bowen had an 18 per cent winning success rate.

The Football Association of Wales believe that, given the circumstances, Toshack performed admirably, but because the national team was so heavily in transition, they were forced to play "safety-first" football and were not winning the key games, which meant crowd figures began to dwindle as a terrible apathy engulfed the side. Finally, after five years as manager, the enormous effort that he had had to put into the rebuilding job took its toll on Toshack. He had clearly lost his enthusiasm, his energy levels fell and he appeared to have put on weight; he was also in a lot of pain owing to a long-standing ankle problem and these difficulties began to filter through to the dressing room.

Wales had a fairly barren run of results during Toshack's final year in charge, losing to Sweden, Croatia and Montenegro, with just a 5-1 victory over Luxembourg to celebrate. That game against Montenegro in the capital, Podgorica, the first of the Euro 2012 qualifying campaign, held the key to his fate. His team lost 1-0 and on the plane back to Cardiff the following day, September 4, 2010, he informed FAW power brokers that he was quitting. Welsh fortunes plummeted even further when, under the guidance of caretaker manager Brian Flynn, they were defeated 1-0 at home to Bulgaria and battered 4-1 by Switzerland in Basel.

At this stage, the FAW knew they were at crisis point. The national team was becoming something of a laughing stock, the butt of cruel jokes – from those who cared to take an interest, that is. Meanwhile, the majority of the nation had simply switched off, which hurt even more than the jibes. This was one of Wales's darkest hours and for the first time in history they slipped out of the top 100 in the FIFA rankings.

Led by their quietly spoken but highly capable chief executive officer Jonathan Ford, the FAW movers and shakers accepted Toshack's decision to stand aside and set about the task of finding the right man to succeed him, knowing this was probably the most important managerial decision they would make in their lives. They quickly determined it was time to move on with a younger, fresher face. Privately, the name on everyone's lips was Ryan Giggs, for whom the vacancy had perhaps come a little too early – and, after that, Gary Speed.

The FAW, like many other British sporting organizations, are an oft-derided group – blazers only interested in their next free lunch, according to some. Ageing, some of them certainly are, with most of the 29-man ruling council in their sixties, quite a few in their seventies, some in their eighties and even the odd one or two in their nineties. The FAW is a founder member of FIFA, the third oldest Football Association in the world. Most of those currently serving were probably also there at the beginning, some cruelly jest! However, it should be pointed out, for the purpose of balance and fairness, that the majority do an enormous amount of voluntary work for Welsh football, giving up their free time seven days a week to run the various minor leagues and grass-roots associations. Thus much of the criticism is misguided and wide of the mark. Nonetheless, there was a feeling among a pocket of supporters that Ford needed to modernize the organization – bring it into the 20th century, let alone the 21st. This appointment, which they had to get right, would be part of that process.

A small sub-committee of some of the more go-ahead FAW individuals was set up to find the new manager, comprising President Phil Pritchard (who hails from Welshpool in mid-Wales), his deputies Ken Tucker (Merthyr Tydfil) and Trefor Lloyd-Hughes (from the island of Anglesey), and honorary treasurer David Griffiths from the valleys town of Maesteg. They were the principal players on the governing body, the four-man officers' group who voted on key decisions, ranging from the next Wales manager to which TV company should be handed the broadcasting rights to international games. They were joined on this particular sub-group by two others: the north Wales-based duo of Steve Williams and Chris Whitley, chair and vice-chair respectively of the FAW's international committee.

The six men were the driving force behind the appointment of Speed – backed up, naturally, by chief executive Jonathan Ford, whose influence cannot be underestimated. Ford comes from an impressive marketing background, having held down a leading post as European sports sponsorship director for drink giants Coca-Cola over a four-year period. He headed up their operation in the UK and worked closely with leading nations at the Euro 2004 Championships in Portugal.

When interviewed by the four-man officers committee for the chief executive role, Ford enthused about how he wanted the FAW brand, an emblem of a red dragon with a green outline, "on the bedroom wall of every schoolboy in Wales". It was a hugely ambitious aim, given the faltering fortunes of the national team, but Ford saw Gary Speed – good-looking, dignified and with a squeaky-clean reputation – as the poster-boy to help deliver his dream and bring the Welsh people back together again. If Wales could land Speed, Ford determined, they would really start to go places and the branding would appear on bedroom walls everywhere.

Unfortunately, Speed already had a contract with Championship club Sheffield United (he had only been manager for three months) and so the FAW had to be seen to be going through the fair and proper process of interviewing suitable candidates who had thrown their hats into the ring and were instantly available. An initial six-man shortlist was compiled, comprising caretaker manager and Welsh under-21 boss Brian Flynn, former Wales strikers John Hartson and Dean Saunders, their old teammate Chris Coleman and two outsiders: previous Wimbledon FA Cup winner and one-time Northern Ireland manager Lawrie Sanchez and potential left-field appointment Lars Lagerback. He was the Swede who had led his homeland, one of England's old tournament foes, to five consecutive major finals and also coached African giants Nigeria in South Africa for the 2010 World Cup. Lagerback was perhaps the thinking fans' choice for the job, though deep down the FAW really wanted a Welshman.

The question was who. In response to this, Ford drew up a list of questions to pose to each candidate, who would then be marked from three (top) down to zero (bottom) on a variety of subject matters, such as past experience of World Cup qualification, club record, whether they held suitable UEFA coaching badges, football philosophy and, finally, their game plan to achieve success with Wales. The system was only a guide, but it gave the FAW something to work with.

Interviews were duly set up in the homeland, at locations away from prying eyes, and on Monday, December 7, 2010, Flynn, Hartson and Saunders were in turn consulted in a private room at the Feathers Hotel in Ludlow. The following day, at the equally smart Taplow House Hotel in Buckinghamshire, Coleman, Sanchez and Lagerback were handed their opportunity to impress. This particular location was chosen for round two of the interviewing process because both Coleman and Sanchez have properties in the Home Counties, while Lagerback flew into Heathrow from Stockholm that very morning.

At this stage Gary Speed was not formally involved, but there was a growing pocket of support pushing for him on the FAW, a feeling that appeared to increase when the committee found limitations with the majority of the initial group of candidates. Then suddenly it emerged that Speed, the man they really wanted, might be interested in changing jobs.

Sheffield United were struggling, having won just six out of the 18 matches in which Speed had been manager since taking over in mid-August 2010. There were even suggestions that he might lose his position with the Blades, although such a claim is instantly dismissed by Kevin McCabe, the Sheffield United chairman who appointed him. "We were fully confident in Gary's ability to turn things around with us," he says in response. "As with Wales, Gary made a relatively slow start to the job with Sheffield United and results were not great, but we had big belief that it was only a matter of time before the hard work he was putting in behind the scenes with the players would be translated into decent results on the pitch. Just like it clearly happened with Wales."

However, the poor run of results in Yorkshire persuaded Wales there was a potential opening here ... and so they pounced. Ford was tasked with making a formal approach to Sheffield United to speak to their manager and he recalls: "Once that permission was given, I got in my car on a Sunday morning and drove back up to the Feathers to speak in person to Gary, picking up a speeding ticket on the way when I was going over the Brecon Beacons, I might add! I knew the situation Gary was under at Sheffield United and we felt there was clearly a potential opportunity for us there. It became clear he did want the Wales job and almost straight away I was able to draft a contract with him. Gary was so nice and amiable that he broke down barriers straight away when we first met him to discuss the job; greeted us as if we were his best friends. As I got to work with him over time, I quickly discovered that was Gary for you – he was everybody's friend off the field. When he did come on board as our manager, he wasn't just the boss, he was one of us; ready to chat to any member of staff, make a cup of tea for them, whatever.

"In the FAW offices we have a birthday club, where people put in £3 to buy a gift for whoever's birthday it is. Gary was part of that – he wasn't aloof in any way whatsoever, despite his fame. If our employees suddenly decided on a Friday night to all go out for a beer, Gary was there in the pub with them, putting his money behind the bar for drinks for all. He was engaging company.

"With regards the way results were going for him at Sheffield United, we weren't perturbed in the slightest. I just had a view that Gary was more suited to international management than the domestic club game. He was a thinker, a real student of world football, a disciple of modern techniques and tactics, and that sort of approach was better served on players at the elite end of the game.

"Gary was really keen on the job and we put the initial contract offer in front of him, but, as invariably happens in cases like this in football, there was a compensation issue to resolve. Gary had only recently put pen to paper on a three-year deal with Sheffield United and while technically it should be the individual leaving his post who pays the compensation to the employer he is leaving, invariably the cost is borne by the next employer.

"There was a lot of negotiating which took place behind the scenes, conducted in a very professional and articulate manner, but at one point I honestly believed it was just not going to happen. Kevin McCabe was insisting upon a certain figure for Sheffield United, we had agreed a set amount among ourselves we were willing to go to and, to be truthful, we were so far apart and I feared it would all fall through. In the end, though, just as the move for Gary's services seemed like collapsing, I was given the go-ahead to hammer out the deal and we struck an agreement."

The FAW paid Sheffield United £200,000 in compensation – a mere drop in the ocean compared to modern-day football finances but money the cash-conscious governing body responsible for running the game, from the top down to the grass roots in Wales, would have prefered to remain in the principality. As it transpired, this was a win-win situation for everybody. Speed was able to leave Sheffield United with his head held high, they could appoint a more experienced manager in an attempt to avoid the relegation mire, the FAW signed the man they had really wanted from day one and the way he duly went on to transform the national team meant the compensation figure paid out was nothing in comparison.

Speed halved his salary by joining Wales, with his pay going down from an estimated £500,000 per annum to a figure closer to the £250,000 mark. Not exactly insignificant to 99.9 per cent of the British working population, of course but in football parlance, a figure top-level players and managers would almost certainly regard as a small sum. That he was prepared to accept such a significant drop in pay merely underlined to the FAW that they had got the right person. Ford admits: "Whenever we have to speak to a prospective manager, there is a serious financial conversation that does need to take place. We have the turnover more of a Championship club than a Premier League team and any salary we can afford to pay clearly needs to reflect that.

"We will always pay a fair competitive rate but we do have to be mindful of the purse strings because we have a responsibility to, and governance of, football at all levels right throughout Wales. Yet whereas the salary on offer may not have been as high as Gary was more accustomed to at club level, there were other pulls we could offer. Remember, there are only 200-odd international managerial jobs throughout the world and there is only one available with Wales. While I fully understand how powerful club football has become, I'd like to think that the international game still has fantastic elements to it. Where did Pelé play his club football, I ask? He is remembered far more for what he did with Brazil in three World Cups than anything he achieved with Santos. Gary was aware of the financial constraints but he told us, 'I'm taking the job because I believe in what I'm doing.' We believed in him, too."

The FAW were additionally able to dangle the carrot of a £1 million bonus, should Speed qualify Wales for the World Cup – a figure which would in effect have paid for itself given the vast commercial opportunities suddenly open to the Dragons, should they manage to join the elite in Brazil 2014. But it wasn't about money, it was about finally ending the Wales qualifying hoodoo and this was certainly the buzz-phrase on Speed's lips as he was officially announced as manager of his country during a press conference at the Vale of Glamorgan hotel on the outskirts of Cardiff on the afternoon of Tuesday, December 14, 2010. Suffice to say, he could scarcely contain his enthusiasm for the challenge that lay ahead.

"I was disappointed to leave Sheffield United because I feel I had unfinished business there, but when your country comes calling, you don't turn them down. In my heart, I know this is absolutely the right decision," he beamed. "The proudest moment of my career was captaining Wales but being manager, the person responsible for the team, will eclipse even that. Having this job is the greatest honour I could have and I'm going to do everything I can to make a success of it. It is my biggest regret in football that I never reached the finals of a major tournament with Wales, so the opportunity to try to put that right and achieve that feat with my country as manager is a challenge I'm ready to embrace with open arms."

On the following day – Speed's first in his new office at the FAW's headquarters, a few miles outside Cardiff city centre – he was soon faced with the harsh realities of international football. An email from FIFA arrived to say that Wales had dipped one place further in the FIFA rankings to 112th, behind those well-known superpowers Guyana, Syria, the Central African Republic and the Cape Verde Islands. Just 24 hours into the job, he hadn't even met his players yet, let alone seen his team kick a ball, and they had fallen further down the world order. The only way is up, they say, but those rankings would actually become worse before they so dramatically improved.

Speed would be first to admit that he inherited gold-dust in terms of playing personnel left behind by Toshack, who had done all the hard work in nurturing a series of gifted Welsh youngsters and giving them international experience from an early age. But they clearly needed a different sort of guidance to hone and fine-tune their budding talents and Gary Speed was just the man to do that.

Where Toshack was old school in his planning and preparation, Speed, by contrast, was much the modern man in his methods. Time for the revolution to begin and he adopted a completely different approach to his predecessor in the way that he tackled the job. First, he took the team away from their traditional Vale of Glamorgan hotel base, their training headquarters for the previous 11 years, opting instead to house them at the smart Celtic Manor resort, which had hosted golf's 2010 Ryder Cup, won so thrillingly by Colin Montgomerie's European side. "I just feel a change of mindset is needed if we are to begin winning matches again and a change of hotel base is part of that. Simple as that," he explained.

Speed demanded that his players turn up for all matches, as he himself always used to do, something that wasn't happening towards the end of the Toshack reign. "Even if they are injured, I want them present to help forge a team spirit and togetherness," he explained. He also insisted they learn the words of the Welsh national anthem, "*Mae Hen Wlad Fy Nhadau*" (Land of My Fathers) and sing them on match day with the same gusto as the Welsh rugby side. Rightly or wrongly, it used to annoy many Welsh fans that their footballers didn't appear to know the words or chose not to sing them, even if they did. As ever in tune with the people, Speed arranged for video clips of the rugby side performing the anthem in stirring fashion at the Millennium Stadium to be shown to his men, explaining he wanted something similar from them. It was even arranged for a former Miss Wales – Courtenay Hamilton, a trained classical singer – to attend those meetings and teach the words phonetically. Speed's belief was that if the players sang the anthem and linked arms at the same time, their actions would display the kind of pride, passion, commitment and unity that many fans felt was lacking.

At the same time, he demanded a move back to the 74,000-seater Millennium Stadium, Wales having quit the home of Welsh rugby prior to his arrival as manager because it was three-quarters empty for soccer internationals and the players regarded this as soul-destroying and merely playing into the hands of visiting teams. "I had some of my best moments at the Millennium, which is among the greatest sports stadia in the world," countered Speed. "I want us to *have* to go back there because we're doing so well it's the only venue big enough to house the amount of people who want to watch us playing."

The biggest change of all, though, was his insistence on Wales embarking on the sports science route, something he had learned from Howard Wilkinson two decades earlier at Leeds and from Sam Allardyce at Bolton. Where Speed lacked Toshack's worldly managerial experience, he made up for this in being as modern and high-tech as possible in his team's preparation for matches, believing the state-of-the-art approach could shake Welsh football from its slumbers and give his side an extra 10 per cent in matches. At the highest level, the impact of that extra help could never be under-estimated, he argued.

One of his greatest friends was Damian Roden, who also happened to be an expert in sports science and had held down jobs with Premier League Manchester City and Blackburn Rovers. Speed immediately hired him as head of performance with the FAW and together they set about implementing a change never before witnessed in the history of the Welsh game. A whole army of backroom staff was brought on board in a part-time capacity, including Craig Bellamy's fitness guru Raymond Verheijen – an outspoken Dutchman who soon became

Speed's official number two and played a big part in helping the manager determine what tactics to adopt, which players to pick and what psychological approach to implement with various individuals.

The system adopted – the "Player Wellness" programme – may have been dismissed as gimmicky by the cynics but Speed was a firm believer in the new approach. In camp, Gareth Bale, Craig Bellamy, Aaron Ramsey and the rest of the Welsh squad were asked to take blood, urine and saliva tests on a daily basis, the results of which were then fed into a computer program. Early each morning, Roden would pore over them to determine exactly what level of fitness each individual player was at and advise Speed and Verheijen accordingly.

Gone was the traditional blanket football approach of yesteryear, where all players gathered for training at 10 a.m., warmed up together, worked out together, did exactly the same routines and invariably finished with a small-sided game. Under Speed, it was specific specialist training for individuals. For example, Gareth Bale was regarded as a thoroughbred by Speed. Like Ryan Giggs for many years before, it was about building him up to a peak on match day, rather than cracking the whip in the run-up. A less talented player such as defensive midfielder Andrew Crofts, on the other hand, could be asked to run through a brick wall at all times.

Speed's argument was that it was not his job to get his players fit – this was the task of their club managers. As far as he was concerned, he must fine-tune and hone elite athletes, allowing them to perform at the peak of their powers come match day. In simplistic terms what he introduced was akin to a traffic-light system. If the results of a blood, saliva or urine test were not good, the player was regarded as being on red and in need of physiotherapy treatment or work in the swimming pool rather than an intensive training session outdoors. Average results were regarded as being on orange and the player's sharpness must be honed on the training pitch. If the results were good, the player was on green but couldn't be pushed too much in case he peaked too early.

The aim was for every player in the squad to be on green by the morning of the match so they would be 100 per cent ready and fully fit for the 90 minutes of football. An army of masseurs and medics was brought on board to help with the Player Wellness programme and there is little doubt the squad warmed to Speed's methods. Nutritionists were also hired to prepare special food and the players instructed to down what a couple of them confided were "horrible-looking coloured drinks" on a regular basis, which they were assured would aid their recovery and performance. Speed even banned room service at the team's hotel to ensure that none of his players stepped out of line and undid all the good work by eating something frowned upon by the nutritionists.

In an explanation of his thought process at the time, he declared: "We're an international team, not a club side. It's not our job to get elite players fit; it's our job to put in place a system which ensures they are in the best possible shape when they are out there on match day. We are leaving no stone unturned in the bid to bring success to Wales. If we've got to conduct the saliva, blood and urine tests and bombard the players with fluids, then that is what we will do. I was always a great believer in sports science when I was a player, feeling it gave me an extra edge and enabled me to play until my late thirties. Some managers might think it's a load of old rubbish, but I believe it's an important tool in football. Even since I stopped playing, the advances in sports science have been huge and we must keep up with the times. You simply have to embrace new ideas because players quickly realize if you are using outdated methods."

Of course theory in football is all well and good but ultimately international management is about one thing: results. It is fair to say they didn't exactly go Speed's way in his early days in charge of Wales. His first match was on February 8, 2011 – away to the Republic of Ireland in the newly formed Carling Nations Cup tournament – which Wales lost 3-0.

The team that night, in a 4-4-2 formation, read as follows: Wayne Hennessey, Neal Eardley, Danny Collins, James Collins, Sam Ricketts, Andy King, Andrew Crofts, David Vaughan, Hal Robson-Kanu, Simon Church and Robert Earnshaw – a team relatively inexperienced at this level and hardly a line-up to strike fear into any international opponent. Thus it came as no real surprise when Wales went down to goals scored by Darren Gibson, Damien Duff and Kevin Fahey, although the somewhat subdued manner in which the team performed did shock a few, given the hard work going on behind the scenes. That night Wales didn't even muster a shot at goal and, interestingly, only two of the starting XI in Dublin – Wolves goalkeeper Hennessey and Norwich midfielder Crofts – were still in the line-up for Speed's final match in charge, eight months down the line.

Fabio Capello's England were next up at the Millennium Stadium, a sell-out 74,000 crowd present to roar on Wales under their new manager in a Euro 2012 qualifier against the Old Enemy on March 26, 2011. As a contest, the game was over after just 14 minutes – the time it took for Frank Lampard to score from a penalty and Darren Bent to add a second, with the Welsh defence sliced apart. Afterwards, Speed looked for the positives by insisting that his players finished the stronger, but things continued to go wrong in the next game as Wales were again defeated, this time 3-1 by Scotland in another Carling Nations Cup tie played in Dublin on May 25, 2011. At least on this occasion Robert Earnshaw did manage to score the first goal of the Speed reign.

Meanwhile, the Welsh players were adamant it was only a matter of time before their results turned round under Speed, with Craig Bellamy describing his time ahead of the England match as "the best week I've been involved in Welsh football". He continued: "I've enjoyed going about my business. We are at a lower point at the moment than for a number of years but it's early days for Gary and he will put his authority on how he wants Welsh football to go forward. He has big views about the future. With Gary, it will be Welsh football first: he wants to leave a legacy and work towards building the biggest moments we have had as a football nation."

Two days after losing to the Scots, Wales recorded their first victory under Speed: an easy 2-0 win over Northern Ireland and once more in a Carling Nations Cup match at the Aviva Stadium, Dublin. It was a low-key affair, played in front of a reported gathering of a mere 529 spectators. Surreal and bizarre, but Speed was finally up and running, with a victory, courtesy of goals scored by Earnshaw again and Arsenal starlet Aaron Ramsey, at just 20 the manager's bold choice as his new captain.

It was back to the bad days, though, in the next match – the lowest point of Speed's tenure – as a Wales team made up mostly of Premier League players including Gareth Bale, Aaron Ramsey and Craig Bellamy lost 2-1 to Australia in a friendly international staged in front of another small crowd at Cardiff City Stadium on August 10, 2011. This was the fourth defeat in five matches played under Speed and there was frustration at how all the hard work going on behind the scenes was not being translated into results on the pitch.

FAW chief executive Jonathan Ford recalls: "I remember the press conference after that Australia game, which was quite painful, if I'm honest. Gary was being asked, 'Is it really coming together as you say it is?' and 'How long do we have to wait for good results, Gary?' He was feeling the pressure at the time and it was an incredibly frustrating period because we knew the atmosphere in camp among the players was fantastic – they loved training and playing under Gary.

"He clearly knew what he was doing, but it just wasn't happening in matches. That said, I never lost faith in Gary – I was going to lots of football matches with him and he could clearly read a game, talking confidently of why a side used a particular structure, why a particular substitute needed to come on (which he invariably did shortly afterwards), and I could see at first hand the hard work he was putting in. He was like a whirlwind, almost in the office 24/7, and I always believed it was only a matter of time before we would start winning matches."

Wales, by this stage, had slumped to an all-time low of 117th in the FIFA rankings. However, Speed appeared to treat these almost with a pinch of salt, often wondering just how FIFA mathematicians came up with the complicated formulae to judge countries. "How do you compare the Cape Verde Islands playing Guyana, with us losing to England?" he asked me. He knew full well that his players and his team were far better than some of the nations oddly placed above Wales in the ratings. Nonetheless, the rankings were significant because FIFA used them to determine the seeding system put in place for the 2014 World Cup qualifying draw. Wales were leapfrogged by the little Faroe Islands and placed down with the also-rans – Andorra, Liechtenstein, Kazakhstan, Malta and San Marino – in the bottom pot of sixth seeds.

It was the ultimate insult for a proud nation which had produced footballers of the stature of King John Charles, Ivor Allchurch, Cliff Jones, John Toshack and Leighton James from yesteryear, as well as Ian Rush, Neville Southall, Ryan Giggs, Craig Bellamy, Gareth Bale, Aaron Ramsey and Speed himself in more recent times. At first Speed tried to play down the importance of the FIFA rankings, pointing out quite rightly: "Look, it doesn't matter if we're in the fourth, fifth or sixth group of seeds. We've got to beat those teams anyway and the second and third seeds, too, if we're to have any hope of qualifying."

But he did concede: "I will admit it's embarrassing. Of course it is. It's embarrassing for me, it's embarrassing for the players, it's embarrassing for the FAW, it's embarrassing for the fans ... There is no getting away from that, no point in trying to bury our heads in the sand about it. But, you know, there is only one way we can do anything about this and that is to go out there and start winning football matches. And fast. Then we will start rising up the rankings again to a position where we all know we deserve to be."

Typically down to earth, very simple and eminently sensible comments from Speed and suddenly the gifted young charges at his command began putting those wise words from their manager into action during a two and a half month spell which saw the most dramatic turnaround of any country anywhere in world football. In those few weeks, the fortunes of Wales were as incredible as their inexplicable dip so low down the FIFA rankings.

The transformation started on a Friday night in Cardiff on September 2, 2011, when FIFA-rated top 20 side Montenegro, who were pushing hard for the Euro 2012 finals to be staged in Poland and the Ukraine after drawing with England at Wembley, arrived in town fully expecting to brush aside Speed's team and pile further qualifying pressure upon Wayne Rooney, Steven Gerrard and Co. That night something stirred inside the Welsh players and, inspired by new captain Aaron Ramsey, who scored one goal and helped set up the other for Steve Morison, Wales triumphed 2-1.

Speed's choice of Ramsey as captain, just 20 at the time and still trying to come back from a broken leg suffered while playing for

Arsenal at Stoke a year earlier, was an inspired one. The easiest thing in the world would have been for him to opt for a more seasoned campaigner such as the vociferous James Collins, who was at the time playing regularly in the Premier League with Aston Villa. But Ramsey, he figured, was there for the long haul and Speed deemed him the perfect figurehead to skipper this gifted young side. Arsenal manager Arsène Wenger argued: "I feel the Welsh job has come a little too early for Aaron. It puts a bit too much pressure on him." However, Wenger did acknowldge that Ramsey would quickly settle into the job and Speed was of the opinion his midfield maestro was a certainty to one day captain Wales, so why not give him the armband from the start, allowing him to grow into the role?

I suspect Speed saw much of himself in the young Ramsey – a midfield playmaker, clean-cut, softly spoken, a potential fixture in the team for the next decade and the perfect ambassador for his country. He wanted Ramsey to be his eyes and ears on the pitch and in the dressing room, just as he himself had been for five years under Mark Hughes.

Ramsey was part of the youthful side that Speed had inherited from Toshack, most players barely out of their teens. But he chose to make it even younger in selecting Swansea City's Neil Taylor at left-back, his club-mate Joe Allen in midfield and Cardiff's Darcy Blake ahead of the more experienced Collins at the centre of his defence. Each could have been a contender for the under-21 team, which meant Speed had the youngest international side in world football under his command, with centre-back Ashley Williams (himself only just into his mid-twenties) positively ancient by comparison.

There's an old adage, though, about youth having no fear, and buoyed by their morale-boosting victory over Montenegro, Speed's Welsh team travelled to Wembley four days later, where they were unlucky to lose to a solitary Ashley Young goal against England. With Ramsey and Bale to the fore and Darcy Blake blotting out the great Wayne Rooney, Wales outplayed Fabio Capello's Three Lions for most of the game. The following morning, any floating supporters – able to watch this particular match on free-to-air television – declared it the best performance they had seen from the Welsh national team for years.

Now the bandwagon really began to roll and Switzerland, who like Montenegro were in the world's top 20 at the time and hopeful of reaching the Euro finals, came to the Liberty Stadium, Swansea, and were expertly dispatched 2-0. That night, Bale, who raced away from the Swiss defence to calmly strike home with a sweet left-foot goal, and Ramsey scored. A few days on, Bale was once more on the score sheet as Wales travelled to Sofia, where they beat Bulgaria 1-0.

"We're really going in the right direction under Gary," enthused Bale. "This is just the beginning – the World Cup in 2014 is our target. Gary is giving us the belief that we're not going into that one just to make up the numbers. Since he came in as manager, we feel we're improving all the time. We want to achieve something special for Wales, and we feel we can do it."

Wales were playing in a style that resembeled Barcelona more than a traditional British team. With Bale wide on the right, Bellamy on the left, and Ramsey and Swansea's Joe Allen pulling the strings so expertly and gracefully in midfield, there was a pace, panache and purpose about their game. They were overpowering teams with the brilliance of their pass-and-move football, with their youth and energy, and with the fast tempo Speed insisted on. Finally, the manager's stamp was there.

Something very special was on the horizon, it seemed, and chief executive Jonathan Ford – never one to miss a marketing opportunity

– was making the most of it. Full-page advertisements appeared in newspapers, as well as posters on the buses with a picture of Speed and the words, "Your manager, your team". The Welsh people were indeed identifying with their young manager.

So too were the players, who, a month after those back-to-back triumphs over the Swiss and Bulgarians, to a man returned to the Welsh camp for the next game: an end-of-year friendly international against Norway at Cardiff City Stadium. Traditionally, such a relatively meaningless fixture leads to a glut of withdrawals, with club managers of the more high-profile stars not wishing them to risk injury ahead of key Premier League games. The fact that not a single Welsh player pulled out on this occasion was a sign of how much they were enjoying their football and preparation for matches under Speed's stewardship. Creating that type of environment was exactly what he had intended. His hand was further strengthened by the knowledge that the team was now winning and his players could be seen walking around the hotel with big, beaming smiles on their faces and a spring in their step.

The Norway game took place on November 12, 2011. It was to be the last time Speed was seen in public in his homeland. Just 15 days later, those youthful players who had placed such faith and trust in their own boyish-looking international manager would learn, one by one, that he was dead. Needless to say, there was not the slightest hint of any problem at the time of the match. On the contrary, Speed – down on the touchline and resplendent in his dark Football Association of Wales blazer, matching tie and crisp white shirt – could be seen punching the air with glee every time his rampant team scored in their resounding and fully merited 4-1 triumph.

It was a sunny afternoon and the pleasant weather conditions, unusual for the time of year, seemed entirely appropriate because the future of Welsh international football appeared so bright under Speed. Early on, Bale set Wales en route for victory by in racing clear of the static Norwegian defence to fire home the opening goal. Bellamy, cutting in from the other side of the pitch, rifled in the second shortly afterwards and super-sub Sam Vokes added a further two near the end.

The scoreline did not flatter Wales in the slightest and the fans, delighted to be entertained by this new-found form, were in jubilant voice. Proudly and triumphantly, they sang the words of the old Andy Williams and Frankie Valli hit "Can't Take My Eyes Off You" – the theme tune which had become the supporters' anthem for the national team back in the early 1990s when Wales were doing well under Terry Yorath, but had rarely been heard at matches since.

The song would at a later date be sang by fans as an emotional tribute to Speed following his death. Indeed when you listen to the lyrics of the original, they are quite apt:

> **You're just too good to be true**
> **Can't take my eyes off you**
> **You'd be like heaven to touch**
> **I wanna hold you so much**
> **At long last love has arrived**
> **And I thank God I'm alive**
> **You're just too good to be true**
> **Can't take my eyes off you.**
>
> **Ba da ba da ba da da ba**
> **Ba da da ba da ba da da**
> **Ba ba da da ba da ba da**
> **Da ba ba da da ba da**

I love you baby
And if it's quite all right
I need you baby
To warm a lonely night
I love you baby
Trust in me when I say …
Oh pretty baby
Don't bring me down I pray
Oh pretty baby, now that I found you stay
And let me love you baby,
Let me love you …

Almost to a person the Welsh people appeared to love Speed. Now they had found him, they wanted him to stay. Any suggestion that he would not remain might have been ridiculed after the Norway match. Deep in the confines of Cardiff City Stadium, Speed held court with the Welsh media, his immense pride at what his team were beginning to achieve shining through as serenely as the spring-like weather that November day.

Wales still had a lot of work to do, he emphasized in typically restrained style. Speed was never one to go over the top when victorious, nor to become overly pessimistic in defeat. There were elements to the team's tactics, he explained, that must be honed before the more important business of trying to reach the World Cup in Brazil began that following autumn. Despite these cautious words, he clearly believed that he possessed a crop of players capable of finally ending the horrendous qualifying jinx. Now the Welsh people were firmly convinced of it, too.

Speed's desire to achieve this aim for his country appeared to burn deep inside him that late afternoon in Cardiff as he talked optimistically to the assembled media about what the future held. After conducting what in the profession is known as his "top table" interview (where managers sit in front of the media and answer questions at an after-match press conference), he then moved to a corner of the room to speak in a more private fashion to a select group of daily newspaper journalists who were looking for a different and fresher angle to the story for the Monday morning papers. When pressed on the extraordinary strides being made by his gifted young guns, Speed made a startling admission which left those of us present somewhat taken aback.

"I would not have got into this Welsh team – I would not have been good enough!" he declared. It was a remarkable statement to make, given that this was a man who had won a record 85 caps for his country as an outfield player, with a League Championship title for Leeds United under his belt, who had shone in the UEFA Champions League with Newcastle and once possessed an array of Premier League appearance and goal-scoring firsts. Noticing the quizzical looks from sports writers, he continued: "No, I'm being absolutely serious. There is quality in this team, from goalkeeper through to centre-forward, which potentially exceeds any Welsh team I have known. They play magnificently together and will get better and better. There are classier players in this team than I ever was and hopefully this is the group who will finally get Wales to one of these major finals. That is certainly my aim."

A whole nation was also starting to genuinely believe because Speed had given them renewed hope. Immediately prior to his arrival as manager just before Christmas 2010, apathy reigned in the principality. The national team may have possessed true Premier League stars such as Bale, Ramsey and Bellamy, but they played pretty much fourth fiddle in Wales, dwarfed by the giant shadow of Warren Gatland's thrilling

Welsh rugby union team and the splendid emergence of Cardiff City and Swansea City as credible football forces at club level.

Match crowds for Wales had been pitiful, interest virtually non-existent, any hopes of qualifying for a major tournament almost at zero level, and to compound matters further, too many players were not even turning up for games. It was a case of the chicken and the egg: Wales were not winning enough ties that mattered so the fans were staying away. Because the fans were staying away, Wales were not winning. On the very first day he was appointed manager, Speed set about changing that mindset. "We need the fans to start coming in big numbers again because the passion they create will help us win matches, but we have to win matches to get those fans back. The two go hand in hand, but it's up to us to do our part of the equation first," he declared. By the time the Norway match was over, the fans were ready to return. Indeed apathy and pessimism had given way to a fresh surge in interest in supporting the boys in red and genuine optimism that the huge strides achieved would be continued under Speed in 2012 and beyond.

Once he had finished his after-match press conference, Speed went up to the players' function room to meet his family. When it was time for the squad to board the team coach outside the main reception of Cardiff City Stadium to take them back to their hotel, there was a slightly unsavoury incident involving Bale and Ramsey, who had recently been photographed posing in Team GB Olympic tops for the London 2012 Games.

A handful of fans had approached the duo and gave them some abuse – a legacy of Wales saying they didn't want their players participating in the Olympics, perhaps? The FAW argument was that taking part as a combined British side would compromise their position as an independent football country. FIFA President Sepp

Blatter insisted there was no danger of this, even penning a letter guaranteeing the future existence of England, Wales, Scotland and Northern Ireland as individual teams and granting them special sanction to appear as a GB side in a one-off at London 2012.

Interestingly, Speed refused point blank to tell Bale and Ramsey they could not play at the Olympics. Always conscious of keeping his best players onside, knowing this represented good modern-day man-management, he said: "I'm not going to tell them what to do. It is their decision and it is up to them."

Back at the team's hotel, Speed said his goodbyes to Bale, Ramsey and the others before they departed for home. Little did anyone realize that this would be the last occasion they would see him alive. There were clearly issues in his private life during the subsequent days, but he again showed little sign outwardly of anything being wrong when, just six days before he death, he flew out to Brussels for a World Cup fixtures meeting with opposing managers of the countries Wales would face in the sprint for Brazil 2014. They were paired with Croatia, Serbia, Belgium, Scotland and a Macedonia side managed by John Toshack, Speed's predecessor in the Welsh post.

As always with these meetings to arrange the order of matches, there was a lot of hard bargaining, but Speed and his number two, Ray Verheijen, were fighting the Wales corner. With so much conflict among the other countries, it seemed that FIFA would have to draw lots to determine the running order. Speed seemed relaxed enough, though, and afterwards lunched with Toshack, whom he later thanked in public for ensuring a compromise sequence of matches was agreed on to suit all parties at the 11th hour.

"Gary seemed fine that day," recalls Toshack. "We talked about Wales, what he saw as the way forward; we had a laugh and joke about various things. All appeared okay on the surface. I was sitting there with him and honestly there didn't appear to be anything troubling him whatsoever, nothing at all. The news that was to then reach us a few days on simply defied belief."

"Speed appeared to be happy enough with Wales's order of matches, saying: "We are in such a well-balanced group it was inevitable everybody would have been looking for a little advantage early on. There had to be some give and take on all sides, but I'm pleased with how it's worked out for Wales. What we need to do is keep our good form going right up to the start of the qualifiers next autumn, and beyond that too."

Toshack was looking forward to the irony of locking horns with Speed and the Wales team he himself had helped to mould in the World Cup qualifiers to come, but the tragic news which came from the Cheshire Constabulary five days later meant that opportunity never arose. The sense of shock and sorrow in Wales at Speed's passing on November 27, 2011 was something previously unseen in British sport. In one terrible moment, the huge bubble of optimism he had built up with his masterful, modern-day management methods was deflated in devastating style.

Twenty-four days after his death was announced, world football's governing body FIFA officially granted Wales the title of Best Mover of the Year. The splendid work Speed had undertaken with his country was recognized further when, before Wales even played another match, they rose another few places to 42nd. No one was left in any doubt that they would have continued their meteoric rise with Speed at the helm and gone on to eclipse the Dragons' best-ever ranking of 29th place – a lofty status achieved when he had just broken into the side as a player himself, back at the start of the 1990s. That is how highly the people of Wales regarded Gary Speed. Their beloved manager had instilled a renewed expectancy and buzz about the Wales national team and finished with a 50 per cent win ratio from his 10 matches in charge, superseding the previous best victory record, held by John Toshack. As with his own life, his period in charge was all too brief and only time could have determined whether the splendid record he set would have become even better.

11

The Legacy

Cardiff City Stadium, Wales: Home Team Dressing Room
Wednesday, February 29, 2012: 7.35 p.m.

It was 10 minutes before kick-off for Wales's first match since Gary Speed's death and Craig Bellamy, stand-in captain on the night (regular skipper Aaron Ramsey was injured), was holding court in the home team dressing room. Pulling the big blue captain's armband over the left sleeve of his red number eight shirt, Bellamy walked to the middle of the room and looked around him. His teammates were now all sitting down on the benches that sweep around the changing room at Cardiff City Stadium, apprehension, anxiety and even bewilderment in their eyes. They were kitted out ready to play in their all-red strip – boots on, shin pads tucked into socks, tie-ups tightened – but this was to be a match like no other and some were naturally wary of what they were about to venture into.

Ahead of them was 90 minutes of football against Costa Rica, a friendly international arranged as a memorial match for the late Gary Speed. The Central Americans had been the first opposition Speed himself had faced in the red of Wales, having made his international debut some 22 years earlier in May 1990, a stone's throw across the road at the old Ninian Park ground. The antiquated home of Cardiff City FC had subsequently been knocked down and replaced by the new stadium, where the Welsh team had begun to play so splendidly under Speed. Just three months earlier, in this very dressing room, he had stood in the same spot as Bellamy, praising his men to the hilt for their performance in battering Norway 4-1.

Now the players had come into camp for the first time since learning of the death of their much-loved manager and they didn't know how they were going to cope. The build-up to the game had been tearful and traumatic enough, but at least they could do their grieving within the privacy of the Welsh team hotel on the waterfront of Cardiff Bay. With just 10 minutes to kick-off, they were expected to walk out in front of a crowd of 23,000 Welsh fans, with Speed's wife, Louise, sons, Ed and Tom, parents, Roger and Carol, and lots of other relatives and friends present, in an attempt to pay a fitting public tribute. Some didn't know how they were going to manage the sense of occasion and Bellamy, realizing he must lead from the front as senior player and the man who had known Speed the longest, understood it was his duty to deliver a pre-match dressing-room pep talk.

During his career, Bellamy had dealt with the pressures of club football at the highest level with Liverpool, Newcastle, Manchester City and Celtic, but he more than most recognized that the demands this time were different. He himself was hurting, having been very close to Speed and given the honour of being one of the pallbearers at his funeral a few weeks earlier. As he stated, he was about to lead out the team into uncharted territory for any footballer; the atmosphere and procedure before kick-off would be different to any other match previously played in. He went on to explain that he didn't know how he was going to cope because he had never been put in this position before, nor did anyone else in that dressing room know for certain how they would react. "But what we've each got to try to do is remember what we've worked on all week and give our best out there. We owe that to Gary," was how he finished his address.

Ashen-faced, he led the others out of the door leading from the dressing room and into the wide tunnel area, where the Costa Ricans were already lined up, as well as match official Howard Webb – the World Cup referee in charge of the game that night. As Bellamy's teammates filed out behind him, there waiting for them in the tunnel were Speed's two sons, Edward and Thomas: Wales mascots for the evening. One was wearing a red Wales number six shirt, the other number 11; each jersey bore the name of their late father. Ed and Tom stood either side of Bellamy at the front of the line and held hands with him. To their right, dressed in a grey suit and unable to play because of injury, was regular captain Aaron Ramsey, who felt he should do his bit by being there on this very special night. As they left the mouth of the tunnel and came in view of the crowd under the bright floodlights, Bellamy, his team and, more importantly, the Speed boys received a rapturous ovation.

Lining up to sing the Welsh national anthem, Bellamy leaned across to offer the youngsters words of support, although at one point he could be seen wiping away a tear from his own face. This was like no other game, a sense of emptiness surrounded the Welsh players, but they were determined to ensure that the Speed family left Cardiff that night content with the whole sense of occasion.

The "giving it our best for Gary" mantra that Bellamy spoke of within the confines of the dressing room had been the basis for how the Welsh team approached the whole build-up to the Costa Rica game – a diktat laid down from the top by Osian Roberts, caretaker boss for the night. Roberts had been Speed's coach and was suddenly left holding the fort as the only senior member of the backroom team still in place by the time the Costa Rica match came around. As technical director of the Welsh Football Trust, the body set up to promote youth development and coaching in Wales, Roberts had taken Speed through his UEFA A Licence badges in the mid-Wales seaside resort of Aberystwyth a few years earlier.

On becoming manager of Wales, Speed remembered those classroom sessions and felt his former teacher could contribute something tangible to the senior international team, even though Roberts himself had never played professional football. Hence, somewhat controversially given his more theoretical as opposed to playing background, Roberts was handed a role as Wales's coach next to Speed and the somewhat outspoken Dutchman Raymond Verheijen. The other key members of the Wales brains trust under Speed were his close friend and sports science expert Damian Roden and operations manager Adrian Davies, a former professional squash player who won 18 world-ranking events and two European Championship titles. Ostensibly his role was to deal with logistical issues, such as which hotel the team would be based at and where they would train; he would also look after any issues among the players.

One by one, each and every one of them other than Roberts himself had left the Wales scene. Roden had gone in September while Speed was still alive, standing aside from his position within the FAW because of what was perceived as a conflict of interest with a drinks firm he was said to have ties with. Davies was an early victim of the post-Speed regime, while Verheijen quit his role as Wales assistant manager in highly contentious circumstances, just days before the memorial match.

Roberts, at least, was still there and was put in charge of the team for the one-off occasion, which included a build-up arguably to be more challenging than the 90 minutes of football itself. "We had been a very close coaching set-up, but suddenly I was all on my own. I realized no one could help me here – I had to do this by myself," he explains. "There was no coaching manual to help me through this one, to advise me how to approach it, because none of us had ever been put in this position before. It almost had to be gut instinct, with one clear overriding factor throughout as far as I was concerned: namely that we had to do something that Gary, and his family, who were at the game, would have been proud of.

"It was a non-football event really, for me. More important was making sure we didn't let Gary down. It wasn't easy being in that dressing room just before kick-off, but then nor had the build-up been easy either. Craig stood up just before we went out and said there were things that were going to happen out there that none of the players had ever experienced before. None of us knew how we were going to cope, but we had to somehow ensure we did our very best. We just had to, for the sake of Gary's memory and the legacy he was leaving behind with this team."

In the event, Wales lost the match 1-0, with a seventh-minute goal from Joel Campbell giving Costa Rica a surprise victory in front of the 23,193 fans who had come to pay their respects. However, the "Don't worry, you gave it your best" speech handed to the players after the game by Gary's eldest son, Ed (as detailed earlier), was enough to satisfy Bellamy and Roberts, captain and manager for the night, that their mantra had at least been adhered to.

Despite the defeat and the sadness of the occasion, it was also a magical evening in its own right, for the Welsh fans made their love of Gary Speed known throughout, chanting his name pretty much non-stop. If there was a sour note, it had come beforehand when the agenda ahead of the Costa Rica clash was dominated by talk of the future concerning Speed's old number two Verheijen, or "Dutch Ray", as he became affectionately known among the Welsh supporters. He had caused outrage in some quarters by going public on the social networking site Twitter a couple of weeks before Christmas (exactly 15 days after Speed's death and barely 48 hours after his funeral) to air his views on the way forward.

"Tomorrow the FAW meet about future of Wales. Hopefully the board will respect Gary's wish, so Osian Roberts and myself can lead the team to Brazil," tweeted Verheijen. "There is no need for a new manager with new ideas; our success was based on Gary's clear structure. Everybody knows what to do for mission Brazil 2014. Months ago, Wales operations manager Adrian Davies sat down with Gary & spoke about the future. He asked him: 'What if?' So we know what to do."

Verheijen was always known for speaking his mind, but even by his standards this was viewed as positively explosive material. His comments, and in particular the 'What if?' remark, were regarded by some Welsh fans as distasteful and quickly seized upon by critical pundits. One of them, former Wales striker Iwan Roberts and an ex-teammate of Speed himself, slammed Verheijen in an interview conducted with the BBC the following morning. "What he put on there [Twitter] really left a bad taste in my mouth," snapped a clearly furious Roberts. "It's just over two weeks since we lost Gary, and just over 48 hours since Gary was finally put to rest. The timing is shocking and I don't think he should be putting his CV, if you like, on Twitter. And what does he mean with that 'What if?' remark?"

Verheijen responded to the flak coming his way by maintaining he had not said that he wanted to be the new manager of Wales but refused, at that stage at least, to comment further, although he was to ruffle a few more feathers in due course. Dutch Ray had evidently become a leading power within the Speed Wales set-up and boasted an impressive CV, having helped managerial great Guus Hiddink coach Holland, Russia and South Korea in various World Cup tournaments. Quite clearly, he was far more than just the fitness and conditioning expert many perceived him to be, having first come to prominence in Wales as Craig Bellamy's mentor, helping the gifted striker iron out the long-standing knee injury problems which had dogged him for many years. The truth of the matter, though, was that the Welsh FA were never going to give the job to Verheijen on a full-time basis, nor indeed to Osian Roberts. Instead, they reflected on the process they had gone through as an interviewing panel only a year prior to the events of November 27, 2011, when they were seeking a successor to John Toshack as manager and had hit upon Speed himself.

Once the shock of Speed's death had begun to subside and a suitable amount of time had passed, including the funeral, those same FAW members formally set about the task of finding a successor; preferably in time for the Costa Rica match, although Verheijen and Roberts could do a one-off game if needs be, but certainly before the beginning of the 2014 World Cup qualifying campaign and beyond. Having so recently gone through the interviewing process, in talks with seven would-be managers, they saw no point in embarking on the same avenue just one year on. Instead, the FAW had a quick debrief about what had happened last time out and hit on two prime candidates: Chris Coleman, who had lost out to Speed by one vote in 2010, and Ryan Giggs, whom Wales had been previously interested in, but for whom the job had come a little too early. Verheijen just wasn't in the mix: it was always going to come down to Coleman or Giggs, but the problem was each was already employed. Coleman was manager of Greek Second Division side Larissa at the time and Giggs of course was still a player with Manchester United, chasing yet another record-breaking Premier League title.

The FAW went about making a formal approach to Manchester United to see if Giggs would be available this time around. If anybody could carry on the splendid work begun by Gary Speed, command the respect of the dressing room, appeal to the fans and help deliver the Wales national team as a marketing man's dream, who better than the greatest modern-day Welsh footballer of all?

Speed had pulled a nation together following the splits that became apparent during the latter days of the Toshack era. Giggs, it was believed, was the man whom most of the Welsh population at large would have identified to continue his legacy. However, married Giggs – who, like Speed, had previously possessed a squeaky-clean image – had recently become embroiled in front-page headlines for the first time in his career. He was famously named in the House of Commons under the protection of Parliamentary privilege by Liberal Democrat MP John Hemmings with regard to a High Court injunction obtained over an alleged affair with reality TV star and former Miss Wales, Imogen Thomas. The resulting bad publicity didn't do Giggs any favours in the FAW corridors of power, where the key decisions about Welsh football are made, but there was a feeling that time would heal everything and the Manchester United legend was still viewed as the prime contender to succeed Speed.

Unfortunately for Wales, any hopes harboured of landing Giggs were quickly dashed as Manchester United were reported to have rejected the FAW's approach and instead swiftly offered him a new playing contract, which would take him to the age of 40. It was also reported that United had ruled out the prospect of Giggs taking the Wales job on a part-time basis for a couple of years and then becoming a full-time manager once he finally hung up his playing boots. Sir Alex Ferguson, the long-serving Old Trafford manager, was already on record as stating it was impossible to play for a club of United's stature with the particular demands and expectations placed on the Old Trafford superstars and manage your country at the same time. So, that was Giggs out of the equation.

When early in the New Year of 2012, the *Western Mail*, the national newspaper of Wales, reported that Chris Coleman was quitting his job with Larissa and strongly linked him with the Welsh manager's post –

the second time the paper had speculated he was the man in waiting – the whole issue of what should happen with Verheijen and Speed's backroom staff once more reared its head. This time around, the ante was upped not so much by Verheijen himself but by Wales captain Aaron Ramsey. The day after the *Western Mail* hinted that Coleman could become the new manager (and thus the writing appeared on the wall for Speed's old backroom team), the young Arsenal midfield star conducted an early-morning radio interview with BBC Five Live, in which he questioned why the Welsh FA had not consulted him or any other player about the way forward. In doing so, Ramsey suggested very strongly that it was his wish to see former assistants Verheijen and Roberts remain to run the show, with a mere figurehead such as Ian Rush brought on board to assist them.

Rush was a highly regarded Welsh scoring legend, with strong links to the Welsh Football Trust organization, which employed Roberts. Whether he possessed the necessary credentials to manage his country or become a so-called figurehead, whatever that meant, was a different matter entirely. Ramsey, it should be emphasized, was not the sort to court controversy. In many ways he was Gary Speed Mark II, more often than not mirroring the diplomatic, dignified manner in which Speed had conducted himself as Welsh captain for seven years. No wonder Speed made him his own skipper – after all, he saw much of himself in young Ramsey. On this occasion, however, Ramsey did not hold back, telling the national radio station: "We don't want to be taking a backwards step again, having a big change and players not wanting to turn up and play for their country. Gary brought in a lot of staff and we had a structure there, we all knew what we had to do and we just want as little change as possible. We've adapted well to the style he and the staff have shown us; we don't want to have a big change now and have to go through that process again."

He continued: "I've spoken to a few of the other players about it and they all feel like I do. We don't want a new manager who is going to bring in a whole new staff with their own styles and techniques. I think someone like Ian Rush, who said that he would just be a figurehead and would support the way we're playing, maybe that would be a good option."

Asked if the FAW power brokers had been in contact, Ramsey replied: "Disappointingly no, they haven't. Obviously in the circumstances I thought they would have contacted myself and a few other players to ask for our opinion." Ramsey's dressing-room colleague Gareth Bale also made his views known, saying that he hoped the FAW would "come to their senses and stick with what we've got".

The FAW in turn were dismissive of Ramsey's remarks. Rightly or wrongly, they deemed the players were the last people they were going to listen to during the search for the new manager. As far as they were concerned, their firm stance was that they were responsible for the governance and running of Welsh football and they were going to make that decision, not the players, who may like one particular manager but perhaps not another.

The following day it appeared the writing was on the wall for Verheijen when the *Western Mail*, under a back-page banner headline "WALES STEP UP MOVE FOR COLEMAN AS THEY IGNORE RAMSEY'S NO CHANGE PLEA", reported that formal talks would begin at once with the now available Chris Coleman, who was back in the UK after his managerial stint in Greece had ended. The newspaper, which clearly had a major in with the FAW, also stated that Coleman would wish to bring his former Welsh centre-back playing partner Kit Symons with him, which would probably spell the end of Verheijen's tenure.

The winds were now firmly with Coleman, but that didn't stop Dutch Ray from once more going public to state that this was not a route the FAW should be taking. He declared the Welsh FA had to respect "Gary's legacy", claiming they would be "turning their back" on him in appointing a new manager and criticizing them for not consulting either himself or Ramsey about the whole process. Verheijen said: "Normally when a manager is sacked, players have to adapt to a totally different way of working when someone new comes in. This is totally different. Obviously, it is a very delicate and sensitive situation but Gary has left behind a successful system. I would hope everyone would understand that all we need is a figurehead to step in; I feel that either Ryan Giggs or Ian Rush would be perfect to fill that role.

"What we don't need is a manager with his own ideas and his own people, because what has been built up could be destroyed over a period of months. If the FAW make that decision, basically they turn their back to Gary Speed and go in a different direction. I think that would be very disrespectful and insensitive. It is also a matter of respecting Gary's legacy, so I think it is the responsibility of the FAW to find the right person who fits in with the current structure and is willing to adapt to the current set-up."

He went on: "It's almost like people don't realize what an incredible improvement the players have made. Given that success, you would expect that the FAW might consult Gary's number two, along with his captain – I haven't spoken with them." Nor was he ever going to. Chris Coleman was duly announced as the new Wales manager on January 20 and on being officially announced at a press conference, he instantly made his views very plain when it came to what he thought of Verheijen and the "figurehead" suggestion put forward by himself and Ramsey.

"I've never met the bloke, nor spoken to him," said Coleman. "If you just need a figurehead, why not get an actor and tell him to be the manager? No, you are either in charge or you aren't. You're either a number one or a number two; you can't have someone in here either acting, or pretending, to be the manager while someone else is doing everything.

"In fairness, Raymond has done a lot of the coaching and the players have responded, but I know football and I know footballers. They have done very well for one man, who isn't here any more. I think some people have forgotten that it was Gary Speed they did well for."

Coleman said of Ramsey: "I'm aware of comments Aaron has made but the tail can't wag the dog," before going on to point out that he planned to retain many of the ideals and football philosophy introduced by Speed, while emphasizing some change under his own management would be inevitable. "There's more than one way to skin a cat," was his way of putting it.

Although the Verheijen issue continued to dominate the agenda, Coleman was more concerned with the fact that he was actually filling the boots of his great friend. He and Speed had roomed together many times while on Wales duty, played with and against one another when they were younger and had developed a close friendship. They had only spoken a couple of times in the last year since Speed was made manager of Wales, he admitted, but they remained good friends.

"When I was given the job that morning before meeting the press, I was first introduced to the full 29-man FA of Wales ruling council," said Coleman. "I told them, 'I'm sorry if I don't appear to be overly enthused or excited about you giving me this role. I am, of course I am – it's the proudest honour, the best job I could have – it's just that I wish the circumstances in which I stand in front of you today had never happened. I want this job badly, but I don't want it in these circumstances. It's bittersweet for me because I was very close to Gary for 30 years and I'm going to miss him."

Indeed, because of the unique circumstances, Coleman decided it was best to stand aside for the Costa Rica memorial match and let Roberts, and possibly Verheijen, take the helm for that game before becoming a more full-time, hands-on manager the following day. That was March 1, St David's Day – in many ways, the perfect timing for a Welshman.

With or without Coleman for Costa Rica, the issue that had bubbled since Verheijen first tweeted about the Welsh managerial vacancy was coming to the boil and did so in the week of the February 29 encounter in the Welsh capital. Seven days before the game, Verheijen was once again on the Twitter warpath, accusing the FAW of being "very disrespectful" in not inviting Adrian Davies, one of the backroom staff members under Speed, to the match. Verheijen tweeted: "I still can't believe the FAW has not invited Team Operations Manager Adrian Davies to be with the team at the memorial game. Very disrespectful." The FAW responded in turn by saying: "Adrian Davies was employed by Gary on a game-by-game basis. He has received tickets for the match, along with hospitality."

Just 48 hours later, and thus five days before the Speed memorial match, Verheijen took to Twitter again to announce that he was quitting his role, in the process taking yet another swipe at the FAW, citing "political and destructive games" as the reason for his departure. "Earlier today I have informed the FAW I will resign," he tweeted. "Have enough of the political and destructive games. Very sad day. Very proud to be part of Fifa's most improved team in 2011."

Some felt Coleman could have prevented all the in-fighting from being dragged out so close to the memorial match by stating publicly from the start that Kit Symons, not Verheijen, would be his number two and thus there would no longer be a role for Dutch Ray. The emotion surrounding the tribute game made that complicated, so Coleman chose to tread a more diplomatic path. Not that it worked, given the contentious circumstances in which Verheijen walked away, anyhow.

The upshot was that with the game fast approaching and the players preparing to come into camp for the first time post-Speed, Osian Roberts found he was on his own and admitted that he was left wondering what to do. "It was such a difficult week," he reflects. "Roger Speed, Gary's dad, had rung me on the Friday night before the game, concerned that Ray had gone. 'You're still going to be involved, aren't you?' he asked. I assured him I would be fine, but his call made me even more determined to make a success of this whole occasion: I wanted Gary's family to feel everything was absolutely right for them. Maybe one day, when I'm older, I will look back upon the night when I was in charge of Wales and think of it as a proud moment but I certainly wasn't viewing it like that at the time, I can assure you. My sole focus was to ensure we prepared for the game and played in a way Gary himself would have been proud of.

"I didn't want to let Gary down; he had gambled on me as part of his coaching team when plenty of questions were being asked about who I was. There is the usual old theory that you need to have been a professional player to become a top coach. Although there are some exceptions to that rule, it was still a big thing for Gary to put his trust in me ahead of the million people he knew in the professional game, people he had played with or under. If we were not successful, there would have been fingers pointed at me as part of the reason. As Gary had placed such confidence in me, I was determined to make sure I didn't let him down in his absence."

Roberts and Speed had forged a close bond during the year they worked together with Wales, having previously crossed paths for the first time in Aberystwyth on the UEFA A Licence course, which Roberts ran as technical director of the Welsh Football Trust. Speed, capped 85 times by his country, captain of Wales a record number of times and having broken Premier League appearance and goal-scoring records, was the football legend but he was very much the pupil to Roberts's teacher during the intensive sessions he needed to undertake in order to gain the relevant qualifications required for modern-day management.

"His thirst to learn and absorb as much knowledge as he could was second to none," recalls Roberts. "When Gary first came down to Aberystwyth to do his coaching badges, he was still a Premier League player at Bolton. The UEFA A Licence, the highest grade you can get, is done in two separate parts and Gary is the only person who took those in successive weeks. Most players will do one part of the course at the end of the season, then understandably want to get away for the summer and do the other part of the course at a much later date, but Gary was so keen to take on board as much information as possible that he decided he wanted to devote all his energies to this in one go.

"Gary's football pedigree spoke for itself, but he quickly realized he had to take a wider perspective on things to make the step up from being just a player to becoming a coach and then a manager. It is totally different to playing the game. When you cross that white line as a player, it's about me, me, me. What's going to get me right to perform to my maximum ability at 3 p.m. on a Saturday? What preparation do I need? What nutrition must I consume, what warm-up routine; when is the best time to have a massage?

"As a manager, you think about everybody in the set-up except yourself: you need to think of the mindset and preparation of all your players and all your backroom staff. It's not just the ones in the starting

XI, you also need to consider the psychology of those players who haven't been picked and how you are going to handle that situation in order to keep them happy and ensure they do not disrupt the team. The last person you think of is yourself and that was a big transition for Gary. As well as obvious technical things such as learning specific coaching drills, he was also suddenly having to ask himself why Sir Bobby Robson, for example, organized training sessions in a particular order or why other managers did X, Y and Z in a particular manner to get the team ready for that 3 p.m. kick-off.

"On the coaching course it quickly became clear one of the things Gary was particularly good at was knowing what his strengths were and, perhaps more importantly, what he was not so good at. Presentation at a team meeting, for example, was a new thing for him and he often looked for feedback there. My response was that it wouldn't come naturally straight away but he would be fine in time – as he was, in due course, it goes without saying."

Roberts may never have played the game at the top level himself, but technically he was the most qualified football coach in Wales and clearly his ideals, vision and inventive modern-day method of doing things had an impact on Speed. With Verheijen, sports scientist Damian Roden and operations manager Adrian Davies, they developed a strong coaching bond.

"We came together not knowing one another, really; certainly never having worked together before," says Roberts. "What we had to quickly develop was an ethos of honesty and trust. We needed to establish quickly that there had to be an openness that we could make criticism if we believed something was wrong, but that it was not criticism of the individual, more of the action. In other words, it was never personal, it was always done for the good of the team; Gary encouraged that. If we thought something he was suggesting was wrong, he wanted us to say so. The last thing he wanted was any of us nodding our heads and just saying 'Yes, Gary,' to everything.

"What we formulated between ourselves was a vision and strategy. Gary knew his remit was the World Cup in Brazil 2014, the qualifiers starting in September 2012, which gave him time – a rare luxury in management these days – to put in place a strategy and a style of play. He said he wanted Wales to be continually competitive and put an end to the ebbs and flows he himself went through as a player. Early on, I remember him telling the players and staff at a team meeting, 'I came close to qualifying for the World Cup in 1993, then we were in the wilderness for 10 years. Then we came close to reaching the Euro 2004 finals before Wales went into the wilderness once more.'

"He explained to us that during that same period of time the Republic of Ireland were the opposite of Wales. 'They either qualify for finals, or at the very least always come close to qualifying. If they can do it, then we certainly can,' was Gary's view."

Roberts accepts that for the first eight months under Speed Wales had struggled, losing four of their opening five matches. "But we all felt that even though the team wasn't winning games, we were winning off the pitch every single time we met up as a squad," he asserts. "Players were turning up for matches, which hadn't always happened before with Wales. We were all eating together; they all wore the same-coloured shirts to meals and to matches. That last point may appear trivial but it was all part of the bigger picture to display the very togetherness Gary demanded.

"Even if players were injured, he asked them to turn up in camp and they began to do so. Why? Because it was a nice environment and they began to realize they needed to attend anyway to ensure they were not left behind the others in terms of tactical development and the video analysis we were doing to plan the way forward. It wasn't always just about the upcoming match itself; Gary even came up with ingenious ideas to cover the differing days he would ask players to turn up. Some were asked to report on a Saturday night, so we could have as much time with them as possible. Others came in on a Sunday, or even Monday because of club commitments or other issues.

"So, how did we make those who came on the Saturday feel it was important they did just that, when they could have looked at others and thought if Sunday was okay for them, why shouldn't it be for me? We would be quite inventive. On one occasion we got a magician in to do a show for them, just something different to make them feel special, to realize that things were being done specifically for them because they had come into camp earlier than others."

Results dramatically turned around, as Speed and Roberts always believed they would, with that off-the-pitch development: four wins out of Wales's next five games prior to Speed's death. The solitary defeat, 1-0 to England at Wembley on September 6, 2011, was a moral victory, too, for Wales played so well that night they deserved at least a draw out of the game when Wayne Rooney was hardly given a kick.

After the 4-1 trouncing of Norway at Cardiff City Stadium towards the end of 2011, things really did look golden for Speed's young team going into 2012. By the time the players next gathered for the Costa Rica match at the same venue, just three months on, that bubble of optimism and hope had well and truly burst. So, how did Roberts cope in handling a squad of 25 players plus other part-time backroom staff still in place, such as physios, masseurs, medics and nutritionists, when the main man they had all grown to like so much was no longer with them?

"It was such a difficult situation," he readily accepts. "We had been in limbo for a while because we didn't have a new manager. Do we carry on the same, or will a new manager bring in his own coaching staff? We had all this uncertainty surrounding us, but at the same time we had the Costa Rica game coming up. We needed to prepare for it and I was determined to ensure we provided a fitting tribute to Gary's legacy. Once the players came into camp, I gathered them together and told them there was no coaching manual I could turn to in order to tell me how to handle this situation, but that over the course of the next few days we had to do our best for Gary's memory. I explained how the Costa Rica match was part of the mission to get to Brazil 2014, which had always been Gary's big aim, and how he would have wanted us to go through with the game."

And get through it they did, even if it was a match like no other they would ever play in, as Bellamy had warned just before kick-off. Wales fell behind to a seventh-minute goal from Costa Rica striker Joel Campbell and try as they might, they just could not claw back the equalizer the Welsh fans longed for in the name of Gary Speed. Not that it really mattered, because pretty much from first minute to last, those supporters continued to sing the name of their former manager throughout. The Speed family would more than likely have been able to drive home to north Wales that night happy with the way the whole occasion had been handled.

FAW chief executive Jonathan Ford says: "It was surprising how many people came up to me and said we were doing things really well. It was a bizarre thing to be complimented on really, but I wasn't pleased for myself – I was more pleased for Gary, knowing he would have been happy with the way we handled everything. Once the Costa Rica match was out of the way, I received a lovely letter from his widow, Louise, and Gary's sister, Lesley, to say thank you to us. That was touching, nice to have. But I did it because Gary was a mate – I just acted from the heart, believing that was the right thing to do."

Which of course was what everyone else tried to do that evening at Cardiff City Stadium: Osian Roberts, the shell-shocked players Speed had left behind, the magnificent Welsh fans responsible for the carnival-like atmosphere, even those of us in the press box, who broke off from working against tight deadlines on our laptops to join in the chanting at times … The job that he had done as manager of Wales and the dignified manner in which Gary Speed conducted himself as a player for 22 years afforded him that level of respect from just about everybody.

So, where does Gary Speed stand among the greats of Welsh football? Talk to supporters and the names of Ryan Giggs, John Charles (the legendary centre-forward of the 1950s and 1960s) and striking sensations Ian Rush and Mark Hughes will always be at the top of the pile. When it comes to iconic managers, it is hard to see the name of John Toshack ever being eclipsed. As well as achieving enormous success domestically, with Swansea City going from bottom of the old Fourth Division to eclipsing Manchester United, Liverpool and Arsenal at the top of the First Division, "Tosh" enjoyed enormous success in a number of countries abroad. You can't imagine another Welshman being twice asked to manage Real Madrid, perhaps still the world's biggest club, an accolade Toshack can proudly add to his CV.

As a player Gary Speed was often understated, but his record-breaking achievements for club and country almost certainly suffice to award him a place in the next batch of all-time greats who come directly after Giggs, Charles and Rush. Managerial-wise, the unfortunate events of November 2011 mean that he simply cannot be properly judged in that category. What can be definitively stated, however, is that in the one year that he was at the Wales helm, Speed won 50 per cent of his matches, making him the best of all time, ahead of his predecessor Toshack, whose own win ratio in the Welsh post stood at 44 per cent. By the same token, the facts and figures show that Speed's losing ratio with Wales (also 50 per cent) was among the worst. Only Bobby Gould (who lost 54 per cent of his matches in charge during the 1990s) and Dave Bowen (defeated in 58 per cent of his games in the 1960s) have inferior records.

As I say, it was too early to judge Speed properly. What had become clear, though, was that his players and the fans had really begun to buy into his ideology with Wales and thus it seems far more likely that things would have got better under his guidance. Of course that can only be conjecture, but my hunch is that his already excellent win ratio would have increased further while his losing ratio may have decreased with more and more games played.

Speed readily accepted and admitted to me on a number of occasions that he had been left a golden crop of young players by Toshack. Instead of having to go through a time-consuming and painstaking rebuilding programme at the highest level, he had inherited a team of teenagers and early-20-somethings who were already experienced international footballers in terms of the number of caps to their names, and also fit and plying their trade week in, week out, in the Premier League. It was a potentially potent cocktail, but they were still in need of fresh guidance. During Toshack's last year at the helm, they had lost their way and at the same time seen their confidence levels dip. Speed set about modernizing the whole set-up and in so doing he also rebuilt the morale of the players, gave them momentum and impetus and led them to four victories out of five prior to his death. If he himself had inherited a wonderful legacy, whoever succeeded him in the post would truly be taking over gold dust. Gifted young players such as Gareth Bale and Aaron Ramsey now felt they were 10 feet tall whenever they pulled on the red of their country as a result of the enormous strides made under Gary Speed.

Like Toshack, Speed believed this was the group of footballers finally capable of ending Wales's 50-plus years' qualifying jinx in getting the Dragons to the finals of a World Cup or European Championships. Of course that achievement would inspire the next and following generations of Welsh players. Playing on that sort of world stage could even bring Welsh international football out of the shadow of rugby union, an extraordinary feat in its own right. With his managerial shrewdness, vision and expertise, Gary Speed had provided Welsh football with real hope and a potentially lasting legacy. He believed that Bale and his teammates could qualify for tournament after tournament, or at the very least become hugely competitive in taking qualification right down to the wire – just as the Republic of Ireland always used to do, a point made early on in his reign.

If, or even when, Wales go on to begin a golden era, Gary Speed will be fondly remembered as one of the key players who set them en route to the other side of the rainbow. Should they fail, whether under Chris Coleman or subsequent managers who succeed him, some fans will argue that the Dragons would have succeeded in the dream had Speed remained at the helm. Conjecture once more, but there are those who remain adamant that under Speed Wales would definitely have broken the 50-year cycle of failure. One thing for sure is that Gary Speed will never be forgotten for what he did for Welsh football, both as a player and as manager of his national team. Even beyond this, his lasting legacy is arguably in how he approached the game, treated everyone with dignity and conducted himself in public with class, politeness and respect … three words that can always be used whenever he is talked about.

The best legacy of all, though, is his two sons, the real stars of that Costa Rica memorial evening. His younger boy, Tom, had walked out with a group of Welsh legends, former teammates of Speed's, who were introduced to the players on the pitch at half-time. Tom spoke into a microphone to tell the enchanted crowd how much he loved to participate in boxing, his preferred sport. By his side was Nathan Cleverly, the World Light-Heavyweight Champion from the Welsh valleys, a big football fan himself.

At the end of the game, Tom's elder brother, Ed, had bowled over the Welsh players with that after-match dressing-room speech of his, when he insisted doing their best against Costa Rica was good enough because that's what his dad had always told him. Earlier in the evening and up in the Redrow hospitality suite, Ed also had the assembled guests in tears when he spoke so bravely about how his family were coping with the tragedy.

"Very mature, lovely young kids," says Osian Roberts, who had got to know the family well. "Tom was into boxing and really good at the sport. Ed broke into my Welsh under-16s squad at the age of just 14 because he was such a good, intelligent young player himself. One of our team administrators once told me he had never met such a polite young boy. Whether you were ringing Ed to tell him about when and where we were getting together, or telling him about meal times, he would always say 'thank you'. They were just great young kids, who wanted to do their father proud."

Speaking to Sky TV in a broadcast which went out shortly before the memorial match, Speed's father, Roger, spoke of how his two grandchildren were following in their father's sporting footsteps and how transporting them to and from venues was helping him to cope: "Watching Ed at football training takes me back to doing it with Gary. I've also got Tommy, who plays for his school team and who does his boxing. It's been a lot easier for me than for Carol because I have been with the boys and a lot has been going on," said Roger.

It is fair to say that both boys did their father proud at Cardiff City Stadium, but Speed will be forever missed by his family, not to mention the Welsh nation and the football family at large. That was Gary Speed's real legacy – everybody seemed to love him, even the millions of fans who didn't really know him as a person outside football. It takes a special man to attract that sort of attention.

RIP, Gary Speed: September 8, 1969–November 27, 2011.

Career Record

Born: September 8, 1969, Mancot, Wales
Died: November 27, 2011, Huntington, Cheshire, England

Playing Career

Leeds United (1988–96)
Signed: June 13, 1988
Debut: May 6, 1989, Football League Division 2, (H) v. Oldham Athletic, drew 0-0
Last match: April 30, 1996, Premier League, (H) v. Newcastle United, lost 0-1

Stats:	Apps	Sub	Goals
Football League	231	17	39
FA Cup	21	0	5
Football League Cup	25	1	11
Other cups:	14	3	2
TOTAL	291	21	57

Honours
Football League (Division 1) Championship 1991-92
League Cup runner-up 1996

Everton (1996–98)
Signed: July 1, 1996, £3.5 million transfer fee
Debut: August 17, 1996, Premier League, (H) v. Newcastle United, won 2-0
   (scored one goal)
Last match: January 18, 1998, Premier League, (H) v. Chelsea, won 3-1 (scored one goal)

Stats:	Apps	Sub	Goals
Football League	58	0	16
FA Cup	2	0	1
Football League Cup	5	0	1
Other cups:	0	0	0
TOTAL	65	0	18

Newcastle United (1998–2004)

Signed: February 6, 1998, £5.5 million transfer fee
Debut: February 7, 1998, Premier League, (H) v. West Ham United, lost 0-1
Last match: April 30, 2004, Premier League, (H) v. Newcastle United, lost 0-1

Stats:	Apps	Sub	Goals
Football League	206	7	29
FA Cup	22	0	5
Football League Cup	9	2	1
Other cups:	39	0	5
TOTAL	276	9	40

Honours
FA Cup runner-up 1998
FA Cup runner-up 1999

Bolton Wanderers (2004–07)

Signed: July 21, 2004, £750,000 transfer fee
Debut: August 14, 2004, Premier League, (H) v. Charlton Athletic, won 4-1
Last match: 9 December 2007, Premier League, (H) v. Wigan Athletic, won 4-1

Stats:	Apps	Sub	Goals
Football League	115	6	14
FA Cup	6	0	0
Football League Cup	4	0	0
Other cups:	5	3	0
TOTAL	130	9	14

Sheffield United (2008)

Signed: January 1, 2008, £250,000 transfer fee
Debut: January 1, 2008, Championship, (A) v. Wolves drew 0-0
Last match: November 25, 2008, Championship, (H) v. Wolves, lost 1-3

Stats:	Apps	Sub	Goals
Football League	37	0	6
FA Cup	2	0	0
Football League Cup	1	0	0
Other cups:	0	0	0
TOTAL	40	0	6

Playing career record:

First match: May 8, 1989, Leeds United v. Oldham Athletic, Division Two
Last match: November 25, 2008, Sheffield United v. Wolves, Championship
Combined transfer value: £10 million

Stats:	Apps	Sub	Goals
Club career	802	39	135

Wales (1990–2004)

Wales Under-21: 3 appearances, 0 goals
Senior Debut: May 8, 1990, Wales v. Costa Rica, Cardiff, won 1-0
Last match: October 13, 2004, Wales v. Poland, Cardiff, lost 2-3
85 appearances (record for outfield player), captain in 44 matches, 7 goals

Key: ECQ = European Championship qualifier; WCQ = World Cup qualifier
*Matches played Anfield while Millennium Stadium was under construction.

Cap

1: May 20,1990: Wales 1 Costa Rica 0 (substitute, friendly, Ninian Park)
2: September 11, 1990: Denmark 1 Wales 0 (friendly, Copenhagen)
3: November 14, 1990: Luxembourg 0 Wales 1 (substitute, ECQ, Luxembourg)
4: February 6, 1991: Wales 0 Republic of Ireland 3 (substitute, friendly, Racecourse Ground)
5: May 1, 1991: Wales 1 Iceland 0 (friendly, Ninian Park)
6: June 5, 1991: Wales 1 Germany 0 (substitute, ECQ, Cardiff Arms Park)
7: September 11, 1991: Wales 1 Brazil 0 (friendly, Cardiff Arms Park)
8: October 16, 1991: Germany 4 Wales 1 (ECQ, Nuremberg)
9: November 13, 1991: Wales 1 Luxembourg 0 (ECQ, Cardiff Arms Park)
10: February 19, 1992: Republic of Ireland 0 Wales 1 (friendly, Dublin)
11: May 20, 1992: Romania 5 Wales 1 (WCQ, Bucharest)
12: May 30, 1992: Holland 4 Wales 0 (friendly, Utrecht)
13: June 3, 1992 Argentina 1 Wales 0 (friendly, Tokyo)
14: June 7, 1992: Japan 0 Wales 1 (friendly, Matsuyama)
15: September 9, 1992: Wales 6 Faroe Isles 0 (WCQ, Cardiff Arms Park)
16: October 14, 1992: Cyprus 0 Wales 1 (WCQ, Limassol)
17: November 18, 1992: Belgium 2 Wales 0 (WCQ, Brussels)
18: February 17, 1993: Republic of Ireland 2 Wales 1 (friendly, Dublin)
19: March 31, 1993: Wales 2 Belgium 0 (WCQ, Cardiff Arms Park)
20: June 6, 1993: Faroe Isles 0 Wales 3 (WCQ, Toftir)
21: September 8, 1993: Wales 2 RCS 2 (WCQ, Cardiff Arms Park)
22: October 13, 1993: Wales 2 Cyprus 0 (WCQ, Cardiff Arms Park)
23: November 17, 1993: Wales 1 Romania 2 (WCQ, Cardiff Arms Park)
24: March 9, 1994: Wales 1 Norway 3 (friendly, Ninian Park)
25: April 20, 1994: Wales 0 Sweden 2 (friendly, Wrexham)
26: September 7, 1994: Wales 2 Albania 0 (ECQ, Cardiff Arms Park)
27: October 12, 1994: Moldova 3 Wales 2 (ECQ, Kishinev)
28: November 16, 1994: Georgia 5 Wales 0 (ECQ, Tbilisi)
29: December 14, 1994: Wales 0 Bulgaria 3 (ECQ, Cardiff Arms Park)
30: March 29, 1995: Bulgaria 3 Wales 1 (ECQ, Sofia)
31: April 26, 1995: Germany 1 Wales 1 (ECQ, Düsseldorf)
32: September 6, 1995: Wales 1 Moldova 0 (ECQ, Cardiff Arms Park)
33: October 11, 1995: Wales 1 Germany 2 (ECQ, Cardiff Arms Park)
34: January 24, 1996: Italy 3 Wales 0 (friendly, Terni)
35: April 24, 1996: Switzerland 2 Wales 0 (substitute, friendly, Lugano)
36: August 31, 1996: Wales 6 San Marino 0 (WCQ, Cardiff Arms Park)
37: October 5, 1996: Wales 1 Holland 3 (WCQ, Cardiff Arms Park)

38: November 9, 1996: Holland 7 Wales 1 (WCQ, Eindhoven)
39: December 14, 1996: Wales 0 Turkey 0 (WCQ, Cardiff Arms Park)
40: February 11, 1997: Wales 0 Republic of Ireland 0 (friendly, Cardiff Arms Park)
41: March 29, 1997: Wales 1 Belgium 2 (WCQ, Cardiff Arms Park)
42: May 27, 1997: Scotland 0 Wales 1 (friendly, Kilmarnock)
43: August 20, 1997: Turkey 6 Wales 4 (WCQ, Istanbul)
44: November 17, 1997: Brazil 3 Wales 0 (friendly, Brasilia)
45: March 25, 1998: Wales 0 Jamaica 0 (friendly, Ninian Park)
46: June 3, 1998: Malta 0 Wales 3 (friendly, Valetta)
47: June 6, 1998: Tunisia 4 Wales 0 (friendly, Tunis)
48: September 5, 1998: Wales 0 Italy 2 (ECQ, Anfield, Liverpool*)
49: October 10, 1998: Denmark 1 Wales 2 (ECQ, Copenhagen)
50: March 31, 1999: Switzerland 2 Wales 0 (ECQ, Zurich)
51: June 5, 1999: Italy 4 Wales 0 (ECQ, Bologna)
52: June 9, 1999: Wales 0 Denmark 2 (ECQ, Anfield, Liverpool*)
53: September 4, 1999: Belarus 1 Wales 2 (ECQ, Minsk)
54: October 9, 1999: Wales 0 Switzerland 2 (ECQ, Racecourse Ground)
55: February 23, 2000: Qatar 0 Wales 1 (friendly, Doha)
56: March 29, 2000: Wales 1 Finland 2 (friendly, Millennium Stadium)
57: May 23, 2000: Wales 0 Brazil 3 (friendly, Millennium Stadium)
58: June 2, 2000: Portugal 3 Wales 0 (friendly, Chaves)
59: September 2, 2000: Belarus 2 Wales 1 (WCQ, Minsk)
60: October 7, 2000: Wales 1 Norway 1 (WCQ, Millennium Stadium)
61: October 11, 2000: Poland 0 Wales 0 (WCQ, Warsaw)
62: March 24, 2001: Armenia 2 Wales 2 (WCQ, Erevan)
63: March 28, 2001: Wales 1 Ukraine 1 (WCQ, Millennium Stadium)
64: June 2, 2001: Wales 1 Poland 2 (WCQ, Millennium Stadium)
65: June 6, 2001: Ukraine 1 Wales 1 (WCQ, Kiev)
66: October 6, 2001: Wales 1 Belarus 0 (WCQ, Millennium Stadium)
67: February 13, 2002: Wales 1 Argentina 1 (friendly, Millennium Stadium)
68: May 14, 2002: Wales 1 Germany 0 (friendly, Millennium Stadium)
69: September 7, 2002: Finland 0 Wales 2 (ECQ, Helsinki)
70: October 16, 2002: Wales 2 Italy 1 (ECQ, Millennium Stadium)
71: November 20, 2002: Azerbaijan 0 Wales 2 (ECQ qualifier, Baku)
72: February 12, 2003: Wales 2 Bosnia 2 (friendly, Millennium Stadium)
73: March 29, 2003: Wales 4 Azerbaijan 0 (ECQ, Millennium Stadium)
74: August 20, 2003: Serbia and Montenegro 1 Wales 0 (ECQ, Belgrade)
75: September 6, 2003: Italy 4 Wales 0 (ECQ, Milan)
76: September 10, 2003: Wales 1 Finland 1 (ECQ, Millennium Stadium)
77: October 11, 2003: Wales 2 Serbia and Montenegro 3 (ECQ, Millennium Stadium)
78: November 15, 2003: Russia 0 Wales 0 (ECQ, Moscow)
79: November 19, 2003: Wales 0 Russia 1 (ECQ, Millennium Stadium)
80: February 18 2004: Wales 4 Scotland 0 (friendly, Millennium Stadium)
81: August 18, 2004: Latvia 0 Wales 2 (friendly, Riga)
82: September 4, 2004: Azerbaijan 1 Wales 1 (WCQ, Baku)
83: September 8, 2004: Wales 2 Northern Ireland 2 (WCQ, Millennium Stadium)
84: October 9, 2004: England 2 Wales 0 (WCQ, Old Trafford)
85: October 13, 2004: Wales 2 Poland 3 (WCQ, Millennium Stadium)

Management Career

Sheffield United (2010)

Appointed: August 17, 2010

First match: August 22, 2010, Championship, (A) v. Middlesbrough, lost 0-1

Last match: December 11, 2010, Championship, (A) v. Barnsley, lost 0-1

Stats:	Played	Won	Drew	Lost	GF	GA	Pts
Football League	18	6	3	9	13	25	21

Wales (2010–11)

Appointed: December 14, 2010

First match: February 8, 2011, Four Nations, (A) v. Republic of Ireland, Dublin, lost 0-3

Last match: 12 November 12, 2011, friendly, (H) v. Norway, Cardiff, won 4-1

Stats:	Played	Won	Drew	Lost	GF	GA	Pts
Euro 2012 Qualifying	5	3	0	2	5	4	9
Four Nations Tournament	3	1	0	2	3	6	3
Friendly	2	1	0	1	5	3	-
TOTAL	10	5	0	5	13	13	12

Game

1: February 8, 2011: Republic of Ireland 3 Wales 0 (Carling Nations Cup, Dublin)

2: March 26, 2011: Wales 0 England 2 (ECQ, Millennium Stadium)

3: May 25, 2011: Scotland 3 Wales 1 (Carling Nations Cup, Dublin)

4: May 27, 2011: Northern Ireland 0 Wales 2 (Carling Nations Cup, Dublin)

5: August 10, 2011: Wales 1 Australia 2 (friendly, Cardiff City Stadium)

6: September 2, 2011: Wales 2 Montenegro 1 (ECQ, Cardiff City Stadium)

7: September 7, 2011: England 1 Wales 0 (ECQ, Wembley)

8: October 7, 2011: Wales 2 Switzerland 0 (ECQ, Liberty Stadium, Swansea)

9: October 11, 2011: Bulgaria 0 Wales 1 (ECQ, Sofia)

10: November 12, 2011: Wales 4 Norway 1 (friendly, Cardiff City Stadium)

Index

Index

Index

Index